CO-CFA-411

JOHN ATKIN

PRACTICAL
SMALL BOAT
DESIGNS

JOHN ATKIN

PRACTICAL SMALL BOAT DESIGNS

INTERNATIONAL MARINE PUBLISHING COMPANY
Camden, Maine

The chapter "Understanding the Lines of a Boat Plan" is based on articles by Jack Davenport that appeared in Boats *magazine, June, July, and August 1955.*

©1983 by International Marine Publishing Company
Typeset by Journal Publications, Camden, Maine
Printed and bound by The Alpine Press, Stoughton, Massachusetts

All rights reserved. Except for use in a review, no part of this book may be reproduced or utilized in any form or by any means, electronic or mechanical, including photocopying, recording, or by any information storage and retrieval system, without written permission from the publisher.

Published by International Marine Publishing Company
21 Elm Street, Camden, Maine 04843
(207) 236-4342

Library of Congress Cataloging in Publication Data

Atkin, John, 1918-
  Practical small boat designs.

  1. Boat-building. I. Title.
VM321.A84 1983   623-8'202   82-48618
ISBN 0-87742-160-9

My work is first dedicated to the treasured memories of my father, Billy Atkin, and the valued heritage he left me. His longtime friend and shipmate William W. Nutting called him the ''Peter Pan of the Sea,'' and I know of few people who realized more ''fun'' in the work of developing over 600 small power and sailing yacht designs.

In addition, my work is dedicated to my wife, Patricia, and my longtime mentor Simon Goldfarb, M.D. Without them, this book would not have been possible.

—— Contents ——

—— Preface ——

While talking with my friend Dudley Slocum down in Nakomis, Florida, one day, he reminded me of having gone to a meeting where I gave a talk on boats. During the meeting someone asked me why I "always designed old-fashioned boats," and I answered, "Because I like them." This amused Dudley, and I suppose it is amusing. But, nonetheless, I do like "old-fashioned" boats. I like their practical design. I like their appearance. I like their character. Perhaps, more than anything else, I like their simplicity — their lack of complications.

Over the years there has continued to be considerable interest in Atkin designs for small "old-fashioned boats" — both my own and those of my late father. Clem Kuhlig's book *Building the Skiff Cabin Boy* (International Marine Publishing Company, 1977) created a truly great amount of interest in this 7-foot 6-inch flat-bottomed rowing and sailing skiff of my design — as well as the 11-foot 4-inch *Nina* and the 10-foot *Flipper*. I have included all three designs in this book.

I continue to make every effort to maintain an open mind — an objectivity — in all matters of yacht design and construction. It is my intention to continue to grow. I do not, however, accept change simply for its own sake. Basically, I am a great believer in the value of tradition — accumulating for use in the present that which has proven best in the past.

I have never been keen about creating "freaks" or incorporating features that I felt were impractical. Nor have I ever been willing to experiment with my clients' money and time.

To be sure, some of my designs have not come up to all expectations, but I am very proud of the many, many letters of thanks that have come along as the years have slid by. It is a rewarding experience, indeed, to read of an owner's pleasure and satisfaction with the performance of a particular boat.

The sea is to be respected — whether you are aboard a 20-, a 40-, or a 400-footer. In my designs I attempt to incorporate a proper proportion of what I feel finds popular acceptance in today's market. But just as important is my inclusion of the fundamentals of wholesome design.

Further, I take seriously the words of my friend the late Sam Rabl: "The designer of any boat for amateur or professional builders carries on his shoulders a grave responsibility."

With these thoughts in mind, I continue to make every effort to design small power and sailing yachts that are at once wholesome, practical, safe, and comfortable.

The process of building a proper wood yacht has evolved over many, many generations, and I have yet to see any breakthroughs, shortcuts, or easy schemes that come close to surpassing traditional methods. I believe the neophyte would do well to explore — and learn — the time-proven methods of the past rather than jump off, half-cocked, into the unknown. You can be certain that countless boatbuilding techniques were used successfully in the past (a visit to the Mystic Seaport Museum will verify this), and it is quite possible to "borrow" from one of these methods in building almost any boat.

I am more and more convinced of the merits of spiling planks, steam-bending frames, and otherwise following traditional construction. Doing so — and utilizing contemporary materials when these have been proven — requires less time and effort than experimentation with the so-called quick-and-easy methods of boatbuilding. Further, I believe the traditionally built boat represents a superior investment in both time and money. I am convinced that it will outlast a boat constructed using any of the "experimental" procedures.

To be sure, it is growing increasingly difficult to find suitable boatbuilding materials. More and more firms are advertising "traditional" boat hardware, however, and materials for the building of a single boat can always be found — one way or another. Two men named Condon and Stevenson built one of our 34-foot double-enders at Los Gatos, California, a good many years ago. By carefully dismantling an old school building, they obtained enough fine yellow pine to fashion the keel, her stem, the planking, and many other structural members. It is this kind of ingenuity that may be necessary from time to time in obtaining materials.

Having personally observed the failures of plywood in numerous instances over the years, I share the opinions held by the late L. Francis Herreshoff, my late father, and other folks who know what they are talking about when they point out its shortcomings. There is no doubt though but that solid-core, waterproof, *marine* plywood, which has been improved by modern adhesives, is pretty much satisfactory. Bruynzeel mahogany, while it is expensive, is simply wonderful material. And products of the United States Plywood Co., developed for *marine* use, stand up surprisingly well. Plywood is particularly well suited for small boats, where it has an opportunity to breathe. The bottom of a flat-bottomed skiff made of *marine* plywood will take a lot of abuse and last a long time. Do not use exterior grade, for this has its shortcomings, but insist that your supplier provide you with true *marine* plywood. Its characteristics will be branded along the edges of the sheets — and do not accept anything else!

Modern Wooden Yacht Construction by John Guzzwell (International Marine Publishing Company, 1979) outlines a good many totally practical approaches to sound construction. With *proven* glues a "cold-molded" hull will last a long time in addition to being enormously strong and light. While it is my feeling that "cold molding" is unnecessarily time consuming compared to traditional boat construction, this is not intended as a criticism.

Today many more folks are finding relaxation, enjoyment and, more importantly, a sense of accomplishment in building their own boat. Further, numerous professional builders of small boats are in quest of proven designs. Judging from the specialized publications and the letters that come along, the building of small boats — quite logically — is viewed as something of an "art form" in addition to being a practical craft.

The *National Fisherman,* the *Small Boat Journal,* and, particularly, *WoodenBoat* magazine provide in their various "how-to" articles a wealth of information on all aspects of wood boatbuilding. Articles written by people such as Bud McIntosh, John Gardner, and other folks "who have been there" are highly instructive.

The increase in the number of boatbuilding schools is another encouraging sign. These schools are generally run by people who are genuinely dedicated to the passing along of a proper way of boatbuilding.

I am continually encouraged by the many letters and photographs I receive from both amateurs and professionals who have turned out a grand piece of work. Many of the amateurs have never built a boat before!

As a prospective amateur builder, you must first select a design that pleases you and fulfills your requirements. When you have expressed confidence in that design, stick to it. Be assured that the competent designer has spent hours, if not days, in his efforts to produce a forthright, practical design. All of the ramifications have been considered carefully. Certainly little changes can (and will) be made to suit individual needs. But you must retain the overall form and fundamental dimensions. The placement of tanks, machinery, and other primary weights must be maintained as shown if you expect to attain any degree of success. And it must be emphasized that any alteration in the design is purely the responsibility of the builder. Rather than taking it upon yourself to increase the length, breadth, draft, etc., of a particular boat, search out a design that suits your needs, be sure that it was prepared by a competent designer, and build that boat in accordance with the plans.

The building of any boat — including those in these pages as well as any others — will, I assure you, provide rich rewards. Her launching day will be long remembered, and after that first delightful afternoon's sail, there will be nothing as satisfactory as when, rowing ashore, you look astern and see your creation tugging at her mooring line. To my knowledge there are no means of expressing the feeling of accomplishment when such a project is completed, nothing that approaches being able to say, "I did it."

In this book, I have attempted to compile a number of simple, practical designs that will make you say to yourself, "I can build that." And have a rewarding experience in the bargain. That is my objective.

John Atkin
Anchordown
Noroton, Connecticut

—— Acknowledgments ——

I want to particularly thank my old friend Ted Smith for the assistance he has given me in tracing various designs.

I also want to thank Richard Orsi for his work in tracing the plans of *Liza Jane, Amos Brown,* and others. Without the help of Ted and Rich, this book would have been far longer in the making.

Thanks to all my friends who sent photographs of the various boats. Special thanks to Captain John Hart, as well as to Bill Colihan, Thomas Massey, F.S. "Sky" Wardwell, Jacob Hess, Charles McNeil, John E. Thomas, and the late James Maze. I sincerely apologize to those whose photographs I neglected to note when they came along.

Thanks, too, to Hearst Marine Books for permission to publish three of the designs.

Nick Philippas, Hildreth Dunn, and Anthony and Com Conti deserve thanks, too, for the interest and time they spent in developing photographs and prints.

Finally, my sincere thanks to all those who have built "little ships" from our designs. Without them, this portfolio would not be possible.

—— Introduction ——

Understanding the Lines of a Boat Plan

"What lovely lines she has!" says the chap sitting on the dock, looking at a contemporary powerboat of "advanced design," that overused term so often applied to streamlined shapes. Undoubtedly, our friend is referring to what is apparent to the average layman: the raking, military mast; the stylish break in the cabinhouses; and the fashionable flying bridge.

In most instances he is overlooking the true "lines" of our hypothetical boat. By definition, the lines are the outlines of a vessel's hull from stem to stern and from keel to sheer. The lines drawing shows the true shape of a vessel, and her ultimate performance depends upon the expert development of her lines.

Unquestionably, the lines drawing is the most important of the drawings involved in a specific design. All the styling involved in the superstructure and rounded deck edges will not cause as much as one-tenth of one percent of difference in the speed of the average powerboat or sailing vessel; it is her lines that will determine her speed, as well as her other characteristics, such as seaworthiness, motion, and dryness. Developing the lines allows the designer to study and analyze the shape of a hull and predict his boat's performance.

In building a successful boat, our task must certainly include both a thorough understanding of the lines drawing and the lofting (or expansion) of those lines to full size on a lofting floor or other smooth surface.

The lines of a little 20-foot cruising sloop accompany these pages in order to illustrate a typical lines drawing in completed form. Indicated in Figure 1 are the body plan (A), the sheer plan (B), and the half-breadth plan (C).

The curved lines in the body plan are called sections and show the shape of the hull where vertical, transverse slices have been taken through it. The curved lines in the sheer plan are called buttocks and show the shape of the hull where vertical, longitudinal slices have been taken through it. In each of the three plans, or "views" of the hull, the "nonoperative" slices appear as a grid of straight lines. The curved lines below the centerline in the half-breadth plan are called diagonals and show the shape of the hull where longitudinal slices have been taken through it at various angles off the horizontal. The diagonals appear as straight lines in the body plan.

In the days prior to "advanced design," and even before the "old-fashioned" hulls of the 1920s, the boat designer (and there were many talented gentlemen pursuing the profession in those times) customarily created his hull shape by building a half model. The half model let the designer (and the prospective builder and owner) see the shape of the boat in three dimensions via a model of one side of her symmetrical hull, scaled down by, say, a factor of 30.

Let's examine the relationship between the "old-fashioned" half model and the "modern" lines drawing.

Imagine, if you will, placing the half model shown in Figure 2 flat (back) side down on a table saw, setting its deck against the miter gauge, and running the hull through the blade at station 6. The resultant shape would be that shown in Figure 3, with the shaded area representing the saw cut. Suppose you were to repeat this performance of sawing through the hull on the various stations from 0 to 12. If you then outlined on paper the "slices" obtained, you'd have a full set of sections like those illustrated in the body plan (Figure 1A) of the 20-footer's lines drawing.

The sections for stations 0 through 6, the forward sections, are drawn to the right of the centerline; the sections for stations 7 through 12, the after sections, are drawn to the left.

A similar hypothetical sawing operation could be carried out for the buttock lines. Setting our imaginary model upright, with its keel on the saw table and its flat side against the rip fence, we run it through the saw in a vertical position on buttock 2 (B 2). The result would be the shaded area exposed in Figure 4. Repeating the process on the balance of the buttocks shown in the lines drawing would allow us to see the exact curves of all the buttocks as shown on the sheer plan (Figure 1B).

Similarly, if the deck of the half model were placed against the rip fence on the saw table and the hull sawn down the load waterline (LWL), the plane revealed would outline the form of the load waterline. Further cuts on the waterline planes both above and below the load waterline (WL 1, 2, etc., and LL 2, 4, etc.) would indicate the forms of the various waterlines. The effect of outlining these plans on paper is shown on the half-breadth plan of the 20-footer (Figure 1C).

To further complicate our sawing operation, we could tilt the saw blade at an angle, while keeping the back of the model against the rip fence, and make more saw cuts in a fore-and-aft direction. If the angle of the blade coincided with the diagonal indicated on the body plan, D 1, the resultant saw cut would expose a surface whose outline is similar to D 1 as illustrated below the baseline in the half-breadth plan (Figure 1C). Similar cuts could be made at the angles of diagonals D 2 and D 3.

There is no limit to the number of sections, buttocks, waterlines, and diagonals possible in a particular lines drawing. The lines shown in Figure 1 present a fairly clear indication of the 20-footer's form. The addition of more lines, however, would provide a further check on the fairness of the hull and would be to the builder's (and designer's) certain advantage. Eventually, the law of diminishing returns comes into play. In any case, the preparation of a lines drawing presents a *far* more accurate means of study than does a half model.

Lofting, or expanding lines to full size, is often viewed by backyard boatbuilders as a great mystery; many builders are very hesitant to undertake this work. The average amateur would rather buy precut templates, paper patterns, or some other device to make building his boat "easy."

I think it is true, however, that if a would-be builder lacks the ability to understand the process of drawing lines full size and going about the work of laying out rabbets, fairing diagonals, and such, he'd best forgo the highly satisfying work of constructing a boat properly. Surely, without the ability to "redraw" the lines drawing, the amateur would have to see the task of building as insurmountable.

It is not uncommon for a builder to lay out only one or two sections (from which mold forms are built) and the outboard profile (sheerline, stem, stern, keel, and garboard), and then proceed to build the boat. But in taking such "shortcuts," he deprives himself of having a good idea of the actual hull form, as defined by the highly essential buttocks, the waterlines, and the diagonals — all of which ought to be properly positioned and faired. There is a strong likelihood that a hull built without full lofting will not be fair.

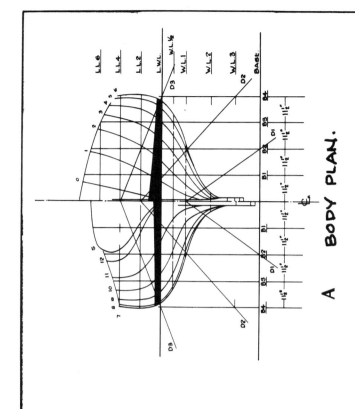

Figure 1. Typical completed lines drawing of a 20-foot sloop, which includes a body plan, a sheer plan, and a half-breadth plan. They indicate the centerline, baseline, sections, sheerline, buttock lines, waterlines, and diagonals.

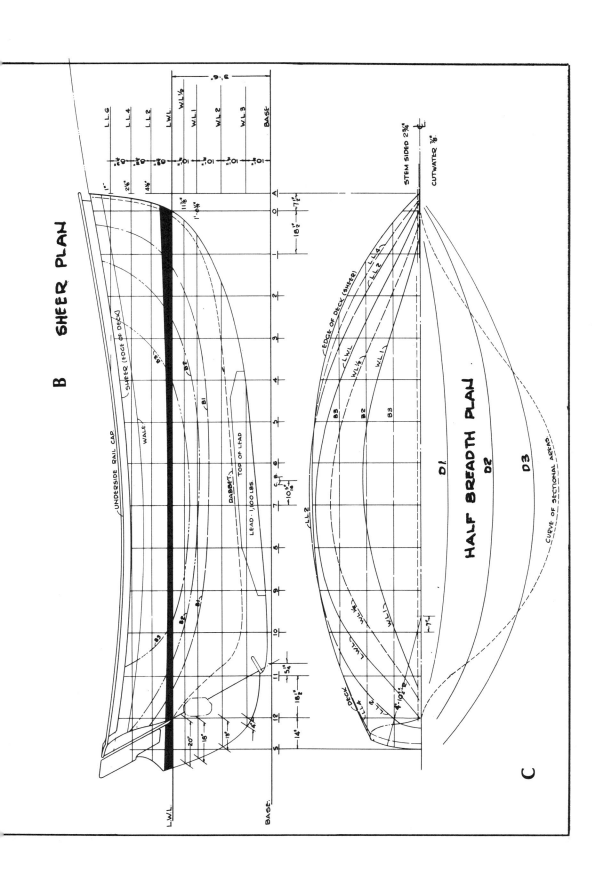

B SHEER PLAN

HALF BREADTH PLAN

CURVE OF SECTIONAL AREAS

C

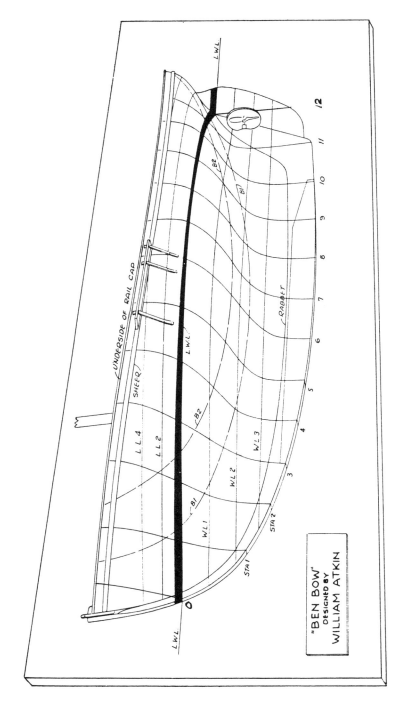

Figure 2. A mechanical perspective drawing showing how the lines develop the shape of a half model and render the contours of the hull. This illustration is not part of the lines drawing, but is used with the text to explain it.

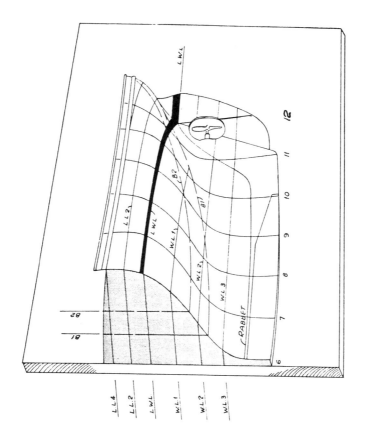

Figure 3. If the half model, as shown above, is sawn through the middle, the cross section (shaded) is revealed.

Figure 4. Another shaded section of the half model, this time through a buttock line.

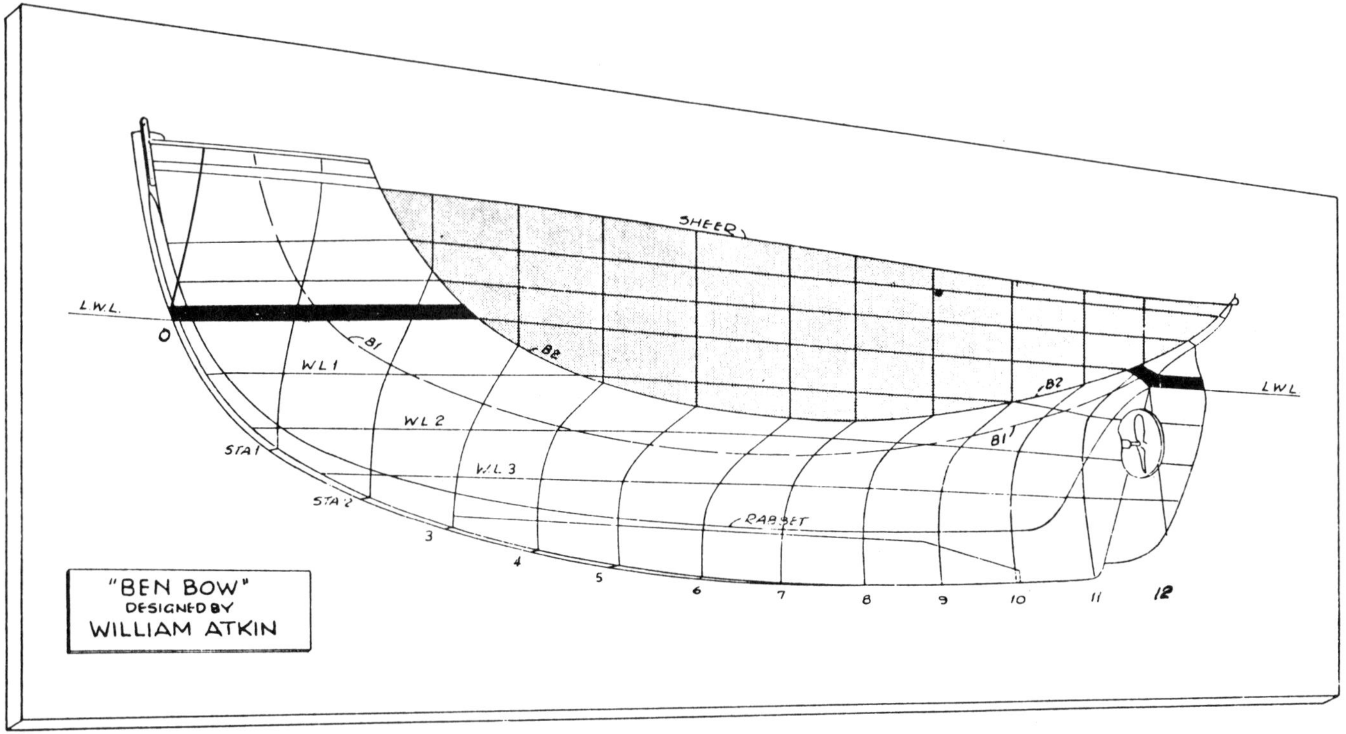

Lofting the lines full size not only provides the builder with a method of duplicating the original small-scale drawings, but also — and more important — tends to correct any errors the designer may have made in the reduced-scale drawings. Lofting generally will "fair up" any inaccuracies in the original lines.

Not only should the lines themselves be drawn full size, but also the construction members, floor heights, engine beds, shaft angles, and other major components. The hours required to do so will, in the long run, be well spent. Further, the laying down of dimensions full size will familiarize the builder with the problems ahead and help him surmount each of these difficulties once the building process starts. The finished, full-size drawings will provide a practical means for the builder to take off templates of the various structural members — stem, knees, horn timber, transom, keel, and so forth. The loft floor will also yield the proper positioning of the rabbet, back rabbet, and bearding line (among others), thus eliminating the necessity of "guessing" at these important features and the risk of spoiling valuable timbers. Another benefit of lofting full size is the possibility of securing all bevels involved in the frames, stem, and other essential points prior to the actual setting-up of these structural members. This alone, in my opinion, more than warrants any and all time involved in the work of laying down lines full size!

Let us now examine the processes of lofting so that the amateur can feel fairly confident in understanding the construction of his dream ship — be she an outboard cruiser of the highest style or a wholesome auxiliary drifting out of the past.

The tools required for the task of lofting the lines consist of the most simple items — one or two carpenter's pencils, a few different-colored pencils, two brad-awls, a wood straightedge about 7 feet long, a steel try-square, a 6-foot rule, a chalkline, chalk, dividers or a compass, a hammer, nails, and various battens.

Now the matter of suitable battens warrants attention. A batten of white pine measuring ⅝ inch square will do nicely for the fore-and-aft lines of a boat up to 25 feet long or so. The length of the batten will depend on the overall length of the hull to be drawn full size; for the greatest convenience, it should extend three or four feet beyond the forward and after stations. Shorter and more limber battens will be required for drawing in the sections of the body plan and for fairing sharp decklines and other curves. All of these will need to be true and normally straight, with any taper made on only one of the edges. With a bit of experimenting, a batten that best suits the curves in question will evolve.

The preparation of a suitable surface upon which to draw the full-size lines must be considered. The lofting floor often presents a problem insofar as space is concerned, but there must be a flat area at least as long as the boat itself and as wide as the full-size half-breadth plan for the vessel. There must also be additional clearance to allow working room.

The surface of this "mold loft" may be the smooth, painted boards of a barn loft or sheets of plywood, Upson board, or Masonite that are properly secured and butted together to present an even, smooth surface. It is advisable to coat this surface with light-colored paint; gray or any tinted white will do nicely, but it must be of flat texture, not glossy. Upson board makes an excellent drawing surface and has the added advantage of being removable, portable, and practical for other uses when the boat is completed.

As mentioned, space limitations normally restrict the size of the lofting surface, or floor, to an area slightly longer than the boat itself and just a bit wider than the expanded half breadth. This means that the three plans in the lines drawing — the body plan, the sheer plan, and the half-breadth plan — must be superimposed as lofting progresses.

Few builders have the luxury of being able to redraw the three plans separately, as in Figure 5A. Instead, the lines are lofted on a practical grid, or network, that can be used in a manner that minimizes the complications of superimposed lines. Such a grid is shown in Figure 5B. This particular boat's sheerline (drawn from the sheer plan) and her deck-edge line (taken from the half-breadth plan) do not conflict or create confusion. Consequently, in the case of this design, it is entirely practical to lay out the lines using a common base and centerline. As the loft work progresses, the process becomes clearer, but it still is good judgment to use a different color for each of the three plans to be expanded on the loft floor.

Figure 6, which includes a standard lines drawing, should clarify the "mysteries" of the table of offsets. This table is a listing of the various dimensions of the boat, as measured (to scale) from the lines drawing. The measurements listed are taken from a baseline to the sheer, rabbet, chine (if any), and so forth — in as simple a form as possible.

Figure 6 shows how the table of offsets functions with the lines drawing. In the sheer plan, for example, the distance from the load waterline to the sheer on station 9 is 2 feet 3⅜ inches. The measurement from the baseline to buttock 2 (B 2) on station 6 is 1 foot 1½ inches. In the half-breadth plan, the distance from the centerline to the deck edge on station 9 is 3 feet 9 inches. The measurement from the centerline to the load waterline at station 6 is 3 feet 6 inches — and so on.

If a small-scale lines drawing indicated all of the dimensions from the load waterline to the sheer, and those from the baseline to B 3, B 2, B 1, the rabbet, the keel, etc., it would become very confused with dimensions (offsets). Consequently, these dimensions are measured from the original lines drawing and entered in the offset table under the proper heading. Each dimension — heights, breadths, and diagonals — is carefully measured and set down until the table of offsets is completed.

In the offset table illustrated, the dimension of 2 feet 3⅝ inches is written as a fraction. Many designers, however, prefer to eliminate the fraction and, instead, enter simply 2-3-5, meaning 2 feet, 3 inches, and 5 eighths of an inch.

Upon completion of the full-size grid and after mastering the concept of offsets, the builder can begin the real work involved in laying down the lines full size. As in so many phases of this business of boatbuilding, expert opinion varies as to the best lofting procedure.

For the purposes of our discussion, the lines of a proven performer have been selected. This little powerboat, whose lines are shown in Figure 5, combines various features rather well. She measures 21 feet 11¾ inches overall by 20 feet 9 inches on her designed waterline. The vessel's breadth is 7 feet 10½ inches, and she draws 1 foot 9½ inches.

Her curved, raking transom, overhanging bow, and round sections will provide a good "case study" upon which to base an explanation of the proper procedures of laying down the lines full size. The principles involved will apply to any hull form, whether large or small, round-, flat-, or V-bottomed. Naturally, each design will mean minor differences in procedure, but by and large, the basic task will apply to any and all vessels.

It should be emphasized that the aforementioned "proper procedures" involved in lofting appear far more complicated than they are. Moreover, the attempt to describe and explain them in detail sometimes only clouds the situation further. Consequently, this would seem an opportune time to recommend that the would-be builder select a design to his liking (or use the hull shown in Figure 5) and redraw her lines to a relatively large scale, perhaps 3 inches to the foot. Carrying out such an exercise will clarify much of what has already been said and provide insight into the problems yet to be discussed.

The lines drawing of any boat, in conjunction with the table of offsets, provides all the necessary dimensions required to draw the lines full size. In instances where the offsets do not include certain specific dimensions, these are customarily shown on the lines drawing, as in Figure 5. Here, for example, the centerline of the rudderstock is indicated at a point 10½ inches abaft station 11, and the centerline of the engine coupling is located 9¾ inches forward of station 8.

At this point, a brief coverage of the terms used in connection with laying down full size may not be out of place.

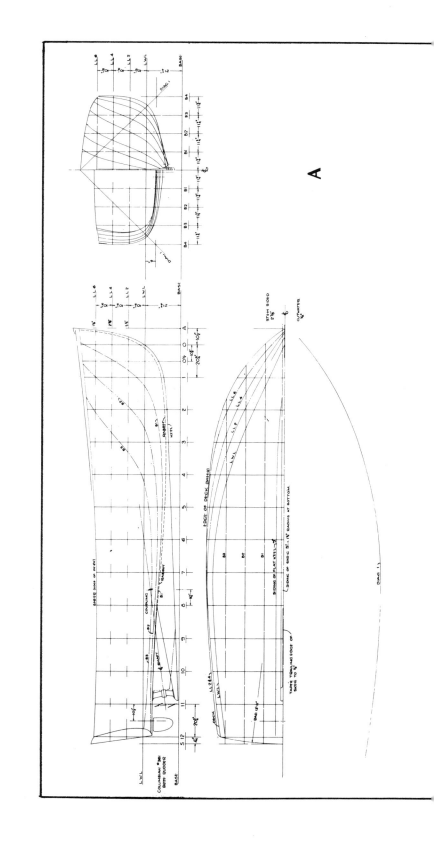

A

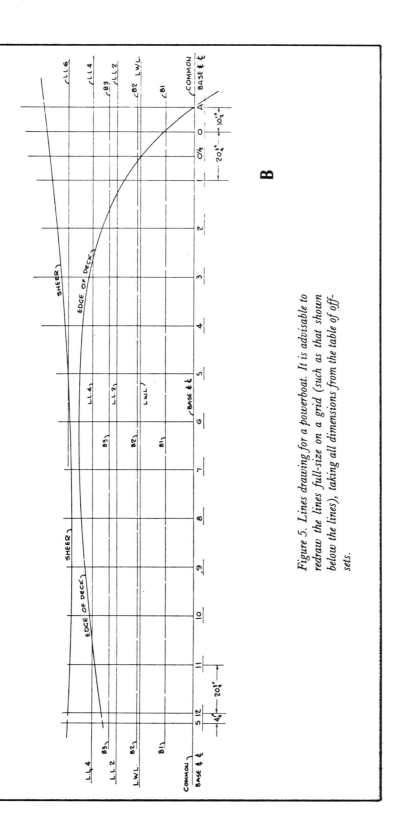

Figure 5. Lines drawing for a powerboat. It is advisable to redraw the lines full-size on a grid (such as that shown below the lines), taking all dimensions from the table of off-sets.

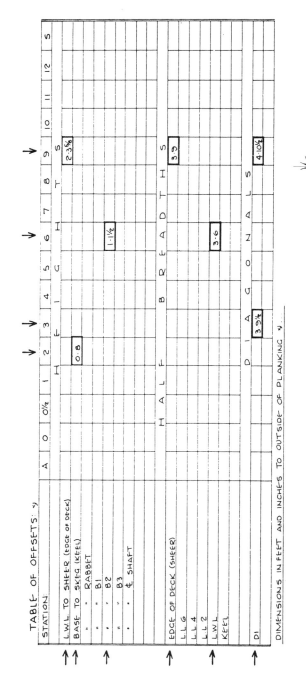

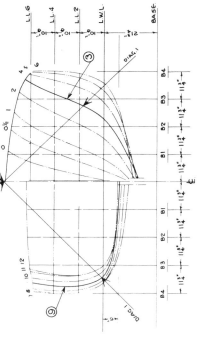

Figure 6. A simple table of offsets that shows some of the typical dimensions and how they are located on the architect's lines drawing. Translation from the table of offsets and the lines drawing to the full-size lofting plan will reveal any mistakes of the architect and provide a fair set of curves to be transferred to the building molds.

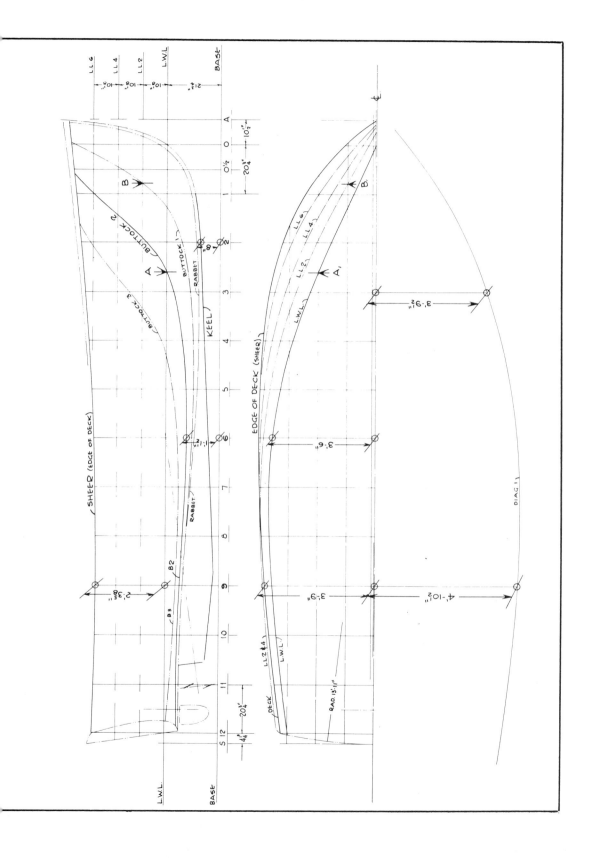

Spots — The points at which any fore-and-aft line intersects with the section lines, or the crossing of any two lines. The marking of offsets on the mold loft floor is to "spot" them.

To pick up (or lift); *to set off* — When the builder has faired the lines in a particular plan and corrected the offsets, it is useful to mark, or "pick up," the final dimensions on a rod or staff so that they can quickly and easily be transferred to, or "set off" on, another plan without the need for further measuring. For instance, when the sheerline has been faired on the half-breadth plan, the distance between the centerline and the sheerline at each station can be "picked up," or marked, on the pick-up rod and then transferred, or "set off," onto the body plan. The rod or staff used for picking up and setting off needs to be rigid enough so that no flexing — and therefore distortion — takes place. The ideal dimensions will obviously vary with the size of the boat being lofted, but a staff measuring ⅝ inch square will suffice for most boats of 25 feet or less. Dimensions marked on the staff may be "erased" with a light plane cut when a particular phase of work is completed. (Picking up, or lifting, is also the term used for transferring the lines of the body plan onto the stock that will be used for sawn frames, but that comes during the construction of the vessel.)

Fairing — A line is fair when it shows pleasing continuity and is free of hollows and humps. The process of fairing involves the correcting of small mechanical errors in the original lines drawing, deviations that become obvious only when the lines are lofted full size. The batten used, for instance, to fair the sheerline in the half-breadth plan is initially bent around the points indicated by the table of offsets. However, when sighting along the batten indicates hollows or flat areas, the batten is "sprung," or set free, and allowed to define a natural, and hence "fair," curve.

Now let's go to work.

It is best if two people work together on drawing the full-size lines, with one reading off the indicated dimensions from the offset table and the other spotting these at the proper height or width of the station in question. When it comes time to run a batten along the spots, one person can sight along it while the other makes the required adjustments in fairing any inaccuracies.

The sheerline, shown in profile as "sheer" in Figure 5, might well be the first of the lines that is laid down. At each station, the sheer height indicated on the table of offsets is marked off above the load waterline (some designers give the sheer heights above the baseline), and a light finishing nail is driven into the loft floor at that point.

The fairing batten is then laid against the nail at station 12 and held in place with another nail driven alongside (not into) the batten, opposite the original nail. The same procedure is repeated at each station, with the batten following the nails (sheer heights) until the entire sheerline is defined. The relatively gentle sweep of this line should cause little difficulty, and the batten should take the curve without trouble.

When the batten is secured, sight along it to see that a fair curve is represented, one that is free of humps, bumps, and irregularities. There is little chance that it will be far off, as long as the designer has made accurate plans. If a mark, or spot, needs raising or lowering to create fairness, pull out the nails in this area, allow the batten to spring in or out, and make the necessary adjustment. Do not attempt to make the change on one station alone, but rather see that the least amount of movement in one or more ''spots'' secures the desired curve. We sometimes learn of dimensions from offset tables being an even one foot off the mark, obviously an error in reading the dimensions from the lines drawing. Use some judgment in these instances, and do not assume there is a sharp break in the sheerline, or that *all* the other dimensions are incorrect. In fact, do not *assume* anything. When you're satisfied with the fairness of the batten, lightly draw the sheerline along it. Proceed with the laying off of the profile: stem, lower edge of keel, rabbet, and transom.

Following the same procedure, using the baseline as a centerline, lay out the proper spots for the edge of deck, fair these up, and lightly mark along the batten the form of the deck in plan. Remember, the half breadths are distances from the centerline to the deckline, to the intermediate waterlines, to the load waterline, and to the siding of the keel. All of these will need to be drawn with great accuracy through their respective ''spots.'' These lines should be drawn lightly because there will have to be further fairing later.

Proceed with the work until the buttocks are ''spotted,'' faired, and drawn in lightly, the single diagonal No. 1 is drawn, and the lines are more or less complete in profile and half breadths as shown in Figure 6.

The body plan may now be drawn. It may be laid out either on a separate, portable panel or directly on the mold loft floor, using station 6 as a mid-section. I suggest doing the body plan separately for clarification as well as for practical use later when the molds will be picked up from the sections. A common vertical centerline is drawn in and the body plan grid is reproduced as shown in Figure 6 with forward stations (sections) 0 to 6 on one side of the centerline and stations 7 to 12 (or S) on the other. As on the half-breadth plan, only half of the body plan is required, since the other side is identical.

Do not use the table of offsets for lofting the sections, but set the offsets aside for the time being, as their usefulness has been fulfilled. From this point *all* dimensions will be "picked up" with a rod, setting off the various distances at each station in their proper position on the body plan. Load waterline to sheer, base to keel, base to rabbet, base to points on B 1, B 2, and so forth, will be picked up from the full-size profile. Centerline to points on LL 6, LL 4, LWL, etc., will be picked up from the half-breadth plan. These points determine the shape of the sections in the body plan. It is essential that the work be done in this manner and that the body plan *not* be drawn directly from the table of offsets. Inquiries received indicate that it is a common error to attempt to make up the body plan from the table of offsets without first laying down the fore-and-aft lines. The body plan *may be drawn in conjunction* with the profile and half breadths, alternating among the three and fairing up as the work proceeds. I feel it is entirely practical, however, to draw all the fore-and-aft lines lightly, fair them, draw the sections from them as described above, and then go about the task of fairing up all lines so they agree in the intersections on all three plans.

The work of fairing will consume some little time and a great deal of thought. In the final fairing process, it is of small matter which lines are faired first, but surely the sheer (in profile) and the deckline (in half breadth) can be considered as established lines, provided they follow closely the dimensions indicated in the offset table with a minimum amount of altering. Lines that cross the grid at nearly right angles, such as buttocks in the after sections or the waterlines in the forward part of the hull, are far more accurate than those that cross grid lines at acute angles.

It is important that additional waterlines and buttocks be added, as required, in the event that a hard or flat spot is indicated. By adding waterlines and buttocks, additional spots may be secured to further fair up the work. Some judgment will have to be used here to reproduce sections similar to those that are drawn in the original small-scale body plan, with each section bearing a resemblance to the original drawing.

The endings of the waterlines warrant special attention, and Figure 7 has been prepared to present this phase of the work clearly. Here the bow profile is drawn, superimposed on the forward part of the half-breadth plan, with the baseline and centerline being common. It is evident from this illustration that the general characteristics of the two plans vary to such a degree that there is no reason for confusion.

To find the forward ending of a waterline in the half-breadth plan, square down from the profile to where the waterline cuts the forward edge of the stem — as, for example, station 0 at the load waterline. This vertical line is projected downward to the point where it crosses the stem, a line offset from the baseline by one-half the width of the forward edge of the stem (in our illustration, this half-siding of the stem is $1\frac{7}{16}$ inches). If the forward edge of the stem broadens at the stemhead, as is often the case, the proper half breadth at the particular waterline (possibly LL 6) must be set out from the centerline.

With the endings of the waterlines established in the half breadths, a reverse operation is undertaken to locate the rabbet line in profile. This has been drawn lightly in accordance with the offsets. By squaring up from the siding of the stem where it crosses a particular waterline in the half-breadth plan, the rabbet line is located on that waterline in the profile drawing. In Figure 7, a line is projected square from the base (centerline) upward from the point of intersection of LL 2 with the half-siding of the stem. The intersection of this projected rabbet line with LL 2 in the profile drawing determines the position of the rabbet on the profile of the stem at LL 2. Similar projections must be made on each waterline in half breadth to its corresponding waterline in profile.

In a similar manner, the back rabbet and bearding lines are established.

These processes appear more complicated than the actual operation, although it must be admitted that considerable accuracy must be achieved in all phases of this "foundation" work of laying down full size.

The expansion of a raking and curved transom, as illustrated in Figure 7, is a fairly involved piece of work. Again, it will be advisable to undertake the work on a small-scale drawing, so as to become familiar with the essential steps. Expanding the transom means projecting its shape as shown in perspective on the body plan to a new drawing showing its "as-built" shape viewed perpendicularly to its line of rake. You do this by working from the sheer plan, however, rather than the body plan.

In the transom sheer plan, the line DR represents the rake of the transom and the centerline for the expanded drawing. From points 1_1, 2_1, and 4_1, where the transom's centerline crosses the waterlines, square down to the centerline of the half-breadth plan. Through each of the resulting intersections on the centerline, draw an arc of a circle, centered on the centerline and using the radius given for the curvature of the transom by the designer (in this instance, 13 feet 11 inches). Also draw a similar arc at station S, which is the deckline (crown is not considered at this time). These arcs may be drawn with a long, stiff batten used as a compass. A nail driven through the batten will act as the pivoting point and a pencil held in a suitable notch will describe the arc.

Where each arc intersects its corresponding waterline, as at A, on LL 2, a point is established indicating the contour of the transom in plan view. These points, as A, squared *up* to the waterlines in profile, establish points 1, 2, and 4 on the LWL, LL 2, and LL 4 from which the curve of the transom, in profile, may be drawn.

Figure 7. The endings of the waterlines are a special problem when laying down the lines full size. The lofting of the curved, raking transom is a complicated but necessary chore. The home boatbuilder will be wise to pick a less difficult form at first.

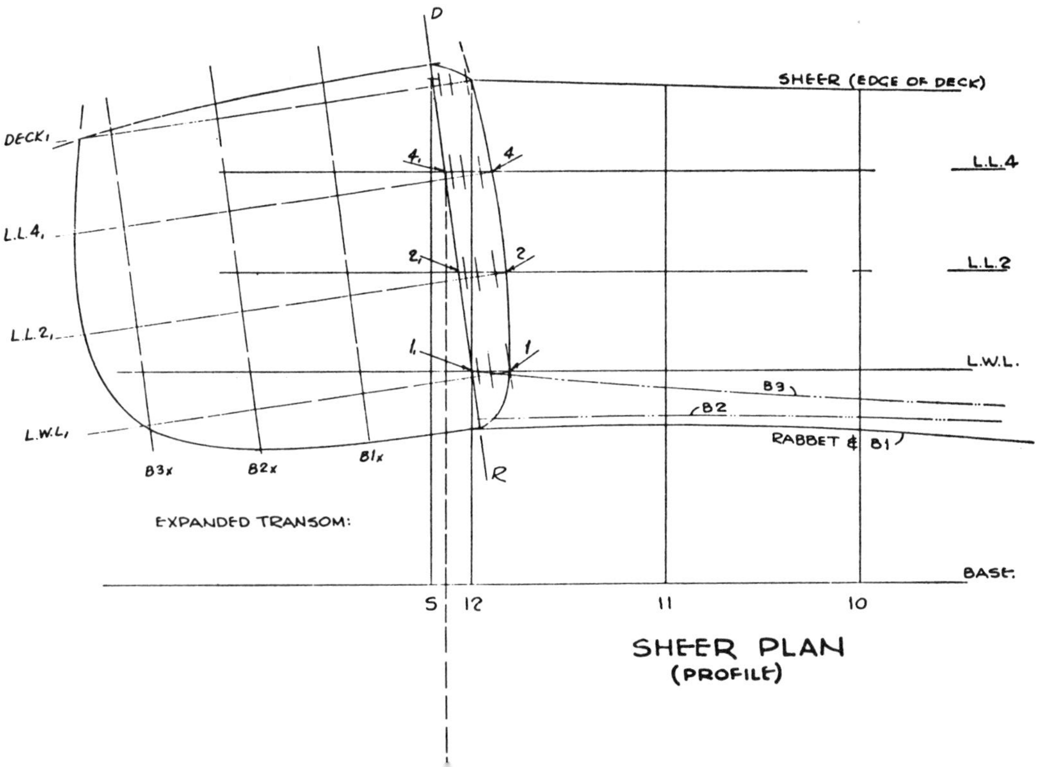

D
SHEER (EDGE OF DECK)
DECK1
L.L.4
L.L.4,
L.L.2
L.L.2,
L.W.L.
L.W.L,
B3
B2
RABBET ℄ B1
B3x
B2x
B1x
R
EXPANDED TRANSOM:
BASE.
S
12
11
10
SHEER PLAN
(PROFILE)

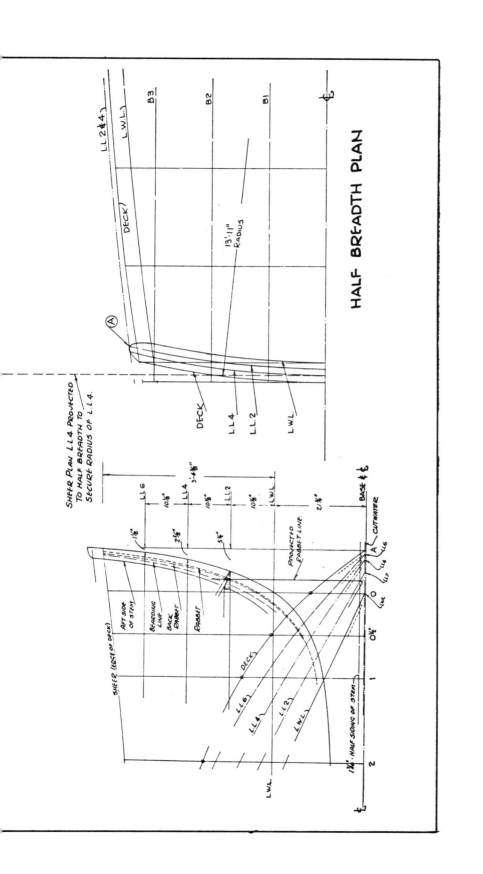

HALF BREADTH PLAN

SHEER PLAN L.L.4. PROJECTED
TO HALF BREADTH TO
SECURE RADIUS OF L.L.4.

13'·11"
RADIUS

LL.2 & 4)
L.W.L)
DECK)
B3
B2
B1

DECK
L.L.4
L.L.2
L.W.L.

L.L.6
10⅜"
L.L.4
3'·4⅛"
10⅜"
L.L.2
10⅜"
L.W.L
2'⅛"
BASE
CUTWATER
A
PROJECTED
RABBET LINE.

1⅛"
2⅝"
5¼"

SHEER (EDGE OF DECK)
AFT SIDE
OF STEM
BEARDING
LINE
BACK
RABBET
RABBET

DECK
L.L.6)
L.L.4)
L.L.2)
L.W.L)

L.W.L.

1¾" HALF SIDING OF STEM

O
O½
1
2

At these points 1, 2, and 4 in the sheer plan, extend LWL, LL 2, and LL 4 at right angles to the rake of the transom (DR). Bend a batten around each arc drawn on the half-breadth plan at the deckline, LL 4, LL 2, and LWL, measuring the distance along these arcs from the centerline to points of intersection with the fore-and-aft waterlines (as A). Lay off these distances, with the batten held straight, on the corresponding waterline extensions perpendicular to the rake of the transom that you drew from points 1, 2, and 4 on the sheer plan. This will establish points LWL_1, $LL\ 2_1$, and $LL\ 4_1$, which will delineate the shape of the side edge of the expanded transom.

On the half-breadth plan, measure the distance between the centerline and each of the buttock lines along the transom arcs you drew. Using these distances, lay off $B\ 1_x$, $B\ 2_x$, and $B\ 3_x$ perpendicular to the waterline extensions on the expanded transom drawing. These buttocks will be spaced very slightly farther apart than those in the half-breadth plan because of the curvature of the transom.

On the half-breadth plan, square up from the intersections of each buttock line with the waterlines on the transom to the corresponding waterlines in the sheer plan. Through the resulting points, draw short lines parallel to the rake of the transom. From the points where the extensions of these lines intersect the buttocks in profile, square over to the buttocks on the expanded transom. The points thus established on the buttocks on the expanded transom will delineate the shape of the lower edge of the expanded transom. You now have six points showing the curvature of the edge of the expanded transom. Additional waterlines may be drawn to secure further points in more accurately determining its form.

The deck crown, an arc, may be drawn from the edge of deck to the rake-of-transom line, DR.

As you can see, some little fussing will have to be undertaken in the work involved in laying down lines full size. It will be time *well spent* in terms of duplicating the design originally conceived by the yacht designer! I hope this brief discussion of lofting will be helpful to the amateur builder. In any case, good luck!

1

——Willy Winship——

14-foot flat-bottomed racing skiff

Willy Winship is a flat-bottomed racing skiff. Her design is based on the excellent and shipshape sailing ''flatties'' made famous by the men who hand-raked shellfish on the Jersey coast some 75 years ago. These boats were smart sailers — able, safe, capable of carrying a good load, and altogether first class.

This is the nature of *Willy Winship,* the boat. Willy Winship, the boy, is a student in the school where my wife teaches art. Like the boat, he is smart, able, and altogether first class — a young man full of vitality and charm.

In designing this youngster's namesake, I wanted first to create a superior kind of boat in which to learn and second to produce an ideal one-design for yacht club use. Furthermore, I thought that she should be a boat that would serve well as a comfortable and safe daysailer.

For this, she had to be driven easily by a low-powered outboard motor and transportable by trailer. Further, it was important that she require a minimum of time and expense on the part of the owner.

Willy Winship is all of these things, and best of all, she can be built for a fraction of the cost needed for a first-class round-bilged or V-bottomed

Sail plan and layout of the racing skiff Willy Winship. *The boat is 13 feet 9 inches overall and is based on the hand raking skiff of the Jersey coast of some 75 years ago.*

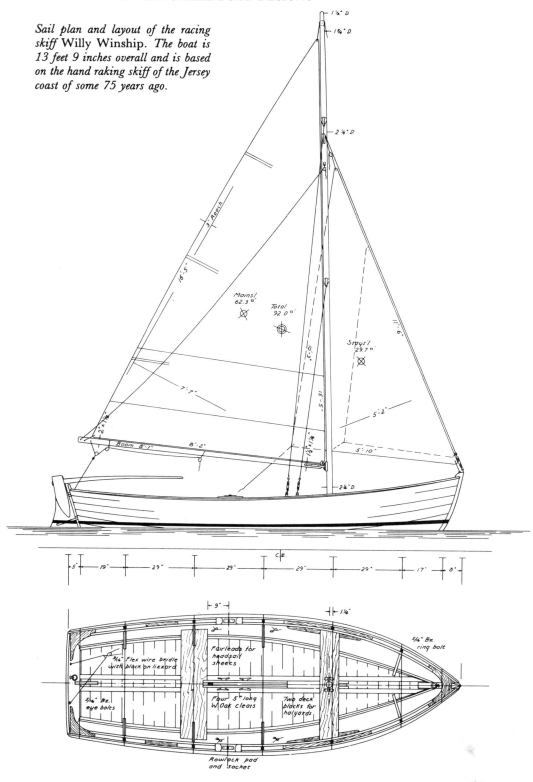

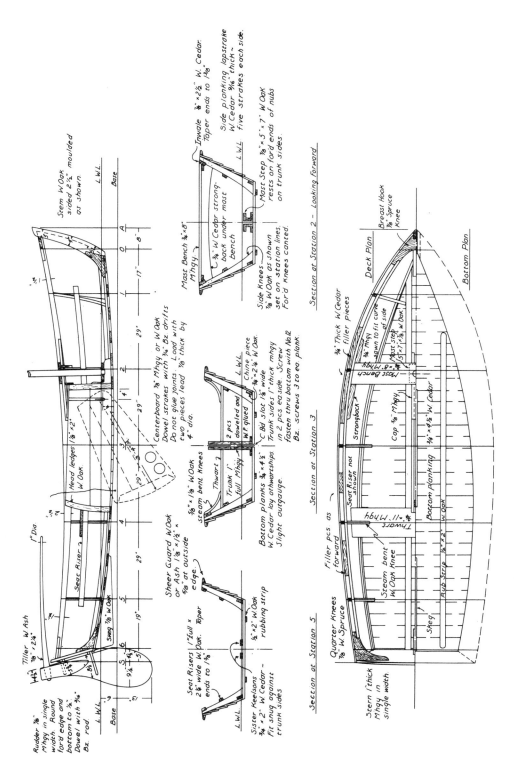

Construction drawings of Willy Winship showing such details as the rudder and centerboard construction; construction of deck plan and bottom; and sections, indicating scantlings. The working drawings include a plywood construction section.

Rudder 7/8"
Mhgy in single
width. Round
for'd edge and
bottom to 1/2".
Dowel with 3/16"
Bz. rod.

Tiller W. Ash
7/8" × 2 1/4"

Stem W. Oak
sided 2 1/2" moulded
as shown

Head ledges 1 1/8" × 2"
W. Oak

Centerboard 7/8" Mhgy or W. Oak
Dowel strakes with 3/16" Bz. drifts
Do not glue joints ~ Load with
two pieces lead 7/8" thick by
4" dia.

Sheer Guard W. Oak
or Ash 1 1/8" × 1/2" ×
5/8" at outside
edge.

Seat Riser

Skeg 7/8" w. Oak

Seat Risers 1"full
2 1/4" wide W. Oak. Taper
ends to 1 1/8"

1/2" × 2" W. Oak
rubbing strip

Sister Keelsons
3/4" × 2" W. Cedar ~
Fit snug against
trunk sides

Section at Station 5

Inwale 7/8" × 2 1/2" W. Cedar.
Taper ends to 1 5/8"

Side planking lapstrake
W. Cedar 9/16" thick ~
five strakes each side

Mast Step 7/8" × 5" × 7" W. Oak
rests on for'd ends of nubs
on trunk sides

3/4" W. Cedar strong-
back under mast
bench

Mast Bench 3/4" × 8"
Mhgy.

Side Knees
7/8" W. Oak as shown
set on station lines.
For'd Knees canted

Section at Station 2 - Looking forward

Chine piece
3/4" × 2 1/4" W. Oak

"C Bd. slot 1 1/8" wide
Trunk sides 1" thick mhgy
in 2 pcs ea. side. Screw
fasten thru bottom with No.12
Bz. screws 3 to ea. plank.

2 pcs
doweled and
W.P glued

Thwart 7

7/8" × 1 1/8" W. Oak
steam bent knees

Trunk 1"
full Mhgy

Bottom planks 3/4" × 4 1/2"
W. Cedar lay athwartships
Slight outgauge.

Section at Station 3

Filler pcs as
forward

Quarter Knees
7/8" W. Spruce

Stern 1"thick
Mhgy in
single width.

Seat Riser not
shown

Steam bent
W. Oak Knee

Thwart 3/4" × 11" W. Mhgy

Rub Strip 1/2" × 2"
W. Oak

Skeg

3/4"Thick W. Cedar
filler pieces

3/4" Mhgy
sawn to fit curve
of side

Strongback

Mast Step
5" × 7" × 7/8" W. Oak

Mast Bench 3/4" × 8" Mhgy

Cap 5/8" M'hgy

Seat Riser 3/4" × 4 1/2" W. Cedar

Bottom Planking
3/4" W. Oak

Breast Hook
7/8" Spruce
Knee

Deck Plan

Bottom Plan

Willy Winship — *full of vitality and charm! (Pat Atkin photo)*

boat of equal dimensions. She thus reflects well the philosophy that was my father's and has also been mine these past 35 years.

I am at a loss to understand the wide acceptance of the present-day "skimming dishes" at numerous yacht clubs. Lacking bearing but abounding in hiking straps and trapezes, these craft hardly qualify as "practical training boats for youngsters." How much more sensible would be a fleet of *Willy Winships,* boats that could show the uninitiated the way of the water — and demonstrate its pitfalls as well.

The many advantages of a flat-bottomed skiff include ease of construction with minimum materials. Little wood is wasted in building such a boat, and fastenings may be galvanized or copper boat nails.

A skiff like *Willy Winship* can be drawn up easily on any reasonably smooth beach and, if grounded, may be gotten off without difficulty or damage. As is the case with most of her type, *Willy*'s interior is easy to clean. The smooth inside of her bottom allows a wooden bailing scoop to be used in quickly freeing the bilge of water. There are no footboards to make or take care of, and interior painting is done easily.

Willy Winship*'s interior
arrangement. The bottom of
the boat is marine plywood,
the topsides lapstrake white
cedar. What a grand piece of
amateur workmanship!*

Do not get the notion that flat-bottomed skiffs are inadequate sea boats
or that they slap and pound. When such boats are heeled over, the sharp
corner formed by the side and bottom acts as an easing V. To be sure, a
flat-bottomed hull will slap under adverse conditions, but this is a small
compromise in light of the numerous advantages!

Willy Winship is 13 feet 9 inches overall, by 12 feet 8 inches on the
waterline, with 4 feet 10 inches beam and 5 inches draft. Freeboard is
1 foot 11½ inches at the bow, 1 foot 1⅛ inches at the lowest point of the
sheer, and 1 foot 4½ inches at the stern. The breadth is carried well forward, while the stern is pulled-in somewhat more than usual. The bottom
is narrow over its entire length. This produces generous flare in the topsides and the assurance of a dry hull, for the combination of the flare and
the plank laps keeps the spray down. She has a big centerboard, which,
unlike a daggerboard, will pivot up in shoal water.

The sail plan shows a total area of 92 square feet with 62.3 square feet
in the main and 29.7 square feet in the staysail. The sails are to be made
of 3.3-ounce Dacron. There should be three battens in the leech of the
mainsail but none in the staysail. If speed and performance are expected,
Willy Winship should have the finest sails made, for they will be the key to
her power.

Working drawings include a plywood construction section showing
⅜-inch waterproof marine plywood on the topsides and bottom. Bottom
frames will extend athwartships.

2

—— Liza Jane ——

19-foot V-bottomed steel knockabout

In 1942, my father prepared the design of this 17-foot 6-inch (waterline length) welded-steel cruiser. I've named her *Liza Jane* at the suggestion of my friend Ed Rogers, who owned a particularly burdensome and wholesome sloop by that name.

The James F. Lincoln Arc Welding Foundation at Cleveland, Ohio, sponsored a design competition that — along with many applications of welding — included watercraft. My father was awarded first prize in this division and received a check for $1,500! He used this godsend, as I recall, toward the construction of Anchordown, our studio/dwelling here in Noroton, Connecticut.

My father's design, as well as many other subjects dealing with welding, are included in a book entitled *Studies in Arc Welding,* which was published in 1943 by the Lincoln Foundation. Over the years, I have received a surprising number of inquiries concerning the *Liza Jane.*

In *Studies in Arc Welding,* Billy Atkin wrote, "With all too few exceptions, small yachts and boats have been built from wood, and most yachtsmen, being conservative, are not easily influenced by the many excellent advantages of metallic hulls.

Liza Jane has a tall mast and a short boom, an altogether efficient rig for a small sailing craft. John Thomas of Englishtown, New Jersey, builder of one of the boats, has written, "I haven't had any serious construction problems — a lot of mistakes but a lot of learning and a great deal of pleasure. My neighbors and friends look upon me with wonder and praise. I would recommend boatbuilding, especially with steel, to anyone with a sagging ego."

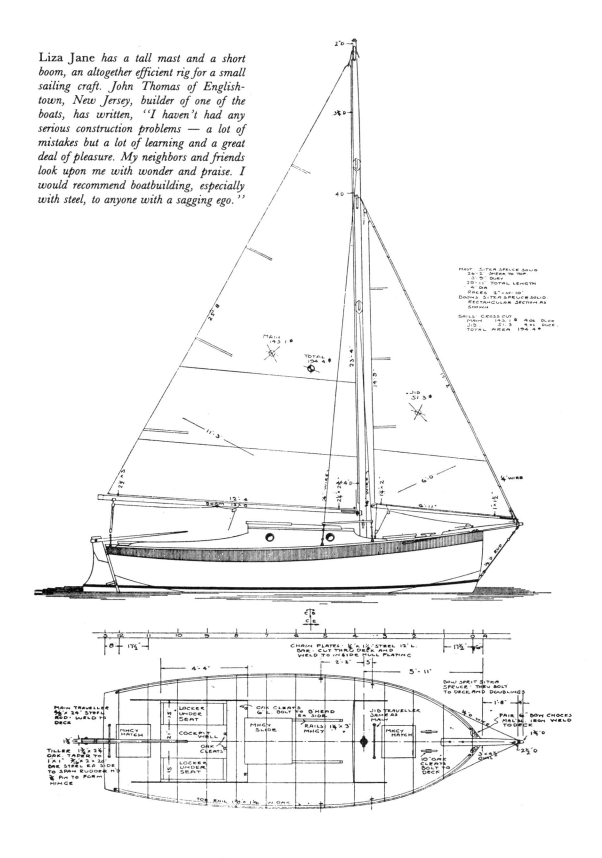

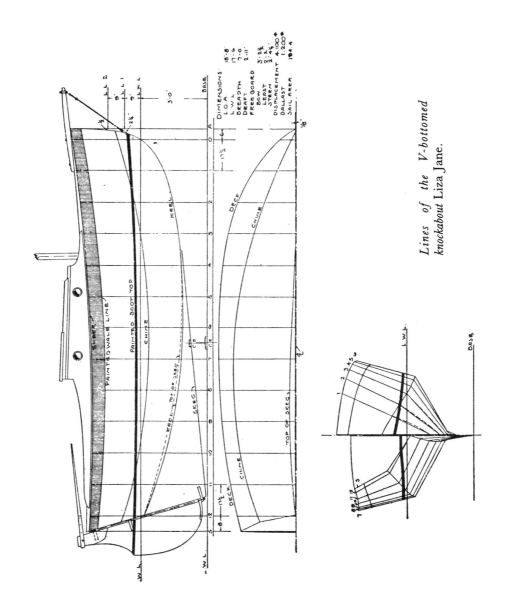

Lines of the V-bottomed knockabout Liza Jane.

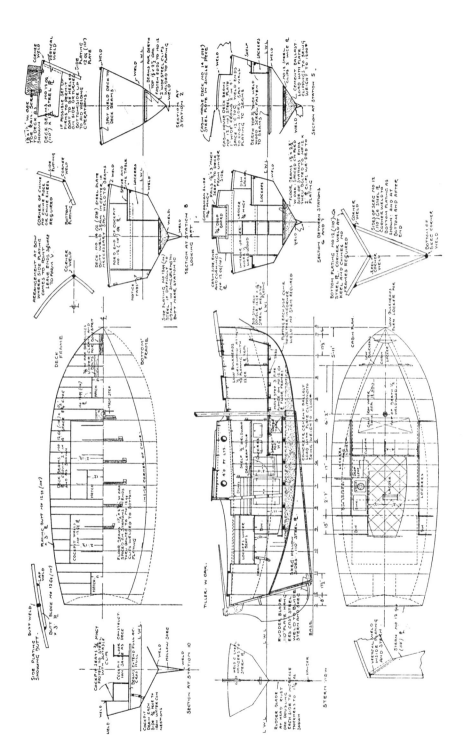

Construction and cabin arrangement of the 18-foot-8-inch-overall Liza Jane. The cabin is designed for the comfort of two, and there is full sitting headroom.

" . . . Mr. W.I. Nichols of Saugus, Massachusetts, has built two small boats adopted from wood construction: one an 18-foot V-bottomed auxiliary designed by the late Charles D. Mower, the other a 23-foot double-ended, V-bottomed runabout from my design. For both these, Mr. Nichols has great praise. Of the latter, he writes that in the hurricane of September 1938, his galvanized Armco iron arc-welded runabout *Needle* was washed ashore before the great wind and tremendous sea, grounding among a forest of jagged boulders and small rocks making up the beach. Except for dents and scratched paint the boat was undamaged structurally.

"Its motor and equipment were ruined with salt water corrosion. Shaft, propeller strut, and rudder were badly bent. Within a week, the iron-hulled *Needle* was about its tasks once again, little worse for her violent experience. Every other of the dozens of small wooden boats that were washed ashore in the locality were smashed into kindling wood, and total losses.

"It is interesting to note that Mr. Nichols' runabout was built from galvanized iron, the decks being approximately $\frac{1}{16}$ inch thick and the sides and bottom plating approximately $\frac{1}{10}$ inch thick. There are no frames, floor timbers, stem, stern, or keel in the construction. Deck beams are the only framing used and these are very light."

Liza Jane is 19 feet 8 inches overall, by 17 feet 6 inches on her waterline, by 7 feet in breadth and 2 feet 11 inches in draft. The displacement is 4,100 pounds; sail area is 194.4 square feet; ballast, all inside, is 1,200 pounds.

My father also noted in his article, "It is difficult for the layman to realize that a hull plated with 12-gauge rolled steel will weigh about the same as a hull planked with three diagonally laid layers of $\frac{3}{8}$-inch white oak, a total thickness of $1\frac{1}{8}$ inches."

He estimated that, including her fastenings, there are approximately 3,495 individual pieces in a wood hull of the nature of *Liza Jane* and a total of only 48 pieces in a steel version. "The above tabulation concerns the hull only, with rudder. However, the interior fitting and rig in either wood or steel hulls will require about the same materials and time to complete."

The topsides of *Liza Jane* are made from 12-gauge steel plate, and the sides may be a single piece. Bottom plating is also 12-gauge steel plate. As mentioned there are no frames. The 1,200 pounds of inside ballast is cement that is loaded with boiler punchings or scrap pieces of plate.

As described by my father: "The cabin is designed for two, and has everything needed for comfortable living and sailing. Provision is made for installation of a pump water closet if this is needed. One cannot expect

The 18-foot-8-inch Liza Jane *nearing completion in the shop of John E. Thomas. The steel hull has been given a priming coat.*

full headroom in a small boat like this, and so long as there is full sitting headroom, the cabin will be found to be snug and comfortable.''

On the subject of steel, I should note that it is well worth considering as a construction material if you have the skills necessary to work it. A few years ago, I was doing a pre-purchase survey in Connecticut on a steel 28-footer that had been built more than 30 years earlier. I was favorably impressed by the amazingly fine condition of the boat. Obviously owned by a meticulous man, the boat was immaculately maintained and showed absolutely no indication of corrosion. (The boat still had its original power plant, and the engine sparkled.) Given proper care, steel boats will last a very long time.

I am pleased to be able to publish this relatively little-known design of my father's with the other practical, small power and cruising boats in this collection. I feel certain it will create favorable interest.

3

—— Shore Liner ——

24-foot flat-bottomed jibheaded sloop

In search of a boat, the late Commander Ed Hanks, of Essex, Connecticut, provided preliminary sketches and outlined his requirements to my father and me. From these, we prepared the design of *Shore Liner*. She and the many sisterships built over the years have proven *Shore Liner* to be an extremely practical, inexpensive cruising boat.

Her principal dimensions are 24 feet overall by 22 feet on the waterline by 9 feet beam and 1 foot draft. There is clear headroom of 4 feet in the cabin, and she is arranged to accommodate two comfortably. The double berth forward is 6 feet 3 inches long. The hatch in the foredeck provides ventilation in addition to emergency escape.

To port and starboard abaft the berths are single upholstered seats, placed there simply to provide a place to sit. Such indispensable conveniences are usually not found in the cabin of small cruising boats. A table hinged on the centerboard trunk completes the comfortable furnishings, which serve well for eating, reading, and working with charts.

Stowage space is provided under the berths, under the cockpit seats, and in the lockers outboard of the counter and starboard seat. The after end of the raised deck cuddy contains the galley. To port, a Primus stove

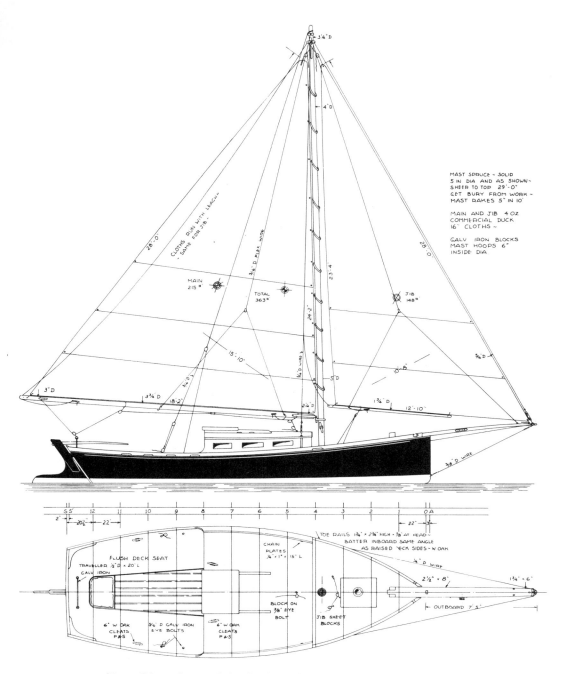

Shore Liner *is one of the simplest sailing cruisers it is possible to build. Like a big, well-designed skiff, she carries a low raised deck, and the low, jibheaded sail plan has proved safe and easy to handle. The mast is arranged in a tabernacle.*

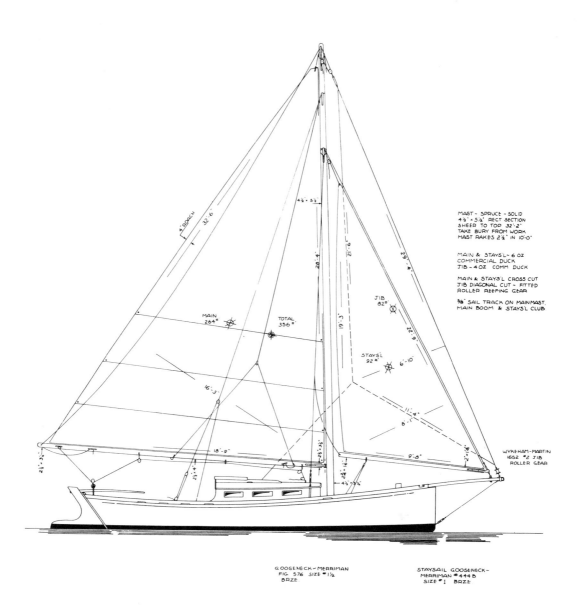

This doublehead rig was prepared for A.R. Dussinger eight years after the original design of Shore Liner *was published. The jib is roller furling.*

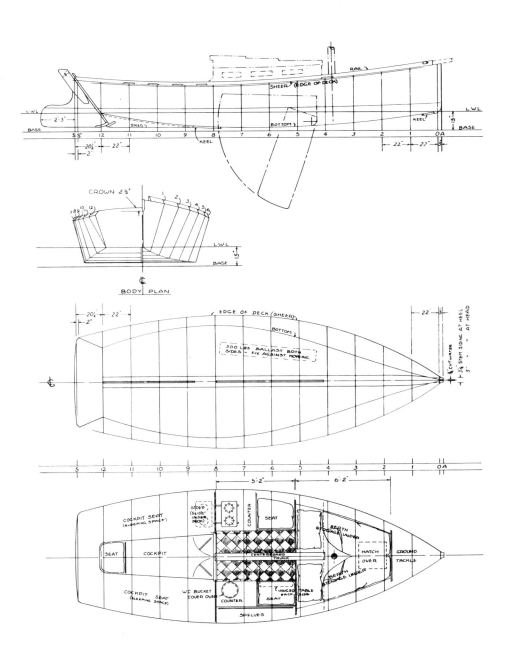

The lines and arrangement of Commander Ed Hanks's 24-foot Shore Liner. *The rails and raised deck are splayed inboard.*

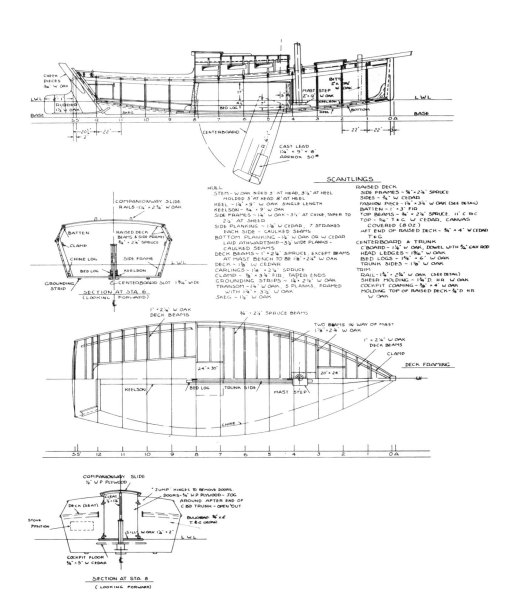

SCANTLINGS

HULL
STEM ~ W OAK SIDED 5" AT HEAD, 3½" AT HEEL
    MOLDED 5" AT HEAD 8" AT HEEL
KEEL ~ 1¼" × 9" W OAK SINGLE LENGTH
KEELSON ~ ¾" × 9" W OAK
SIDE FRAMES ~ 1¼" W OAK ~ 3½" AT CHINE, TAPER TO
    2½" AT SHEER
SIDE PLANKING ~ 1⅛" W CEDAR, 7 STRAKES
    EACH SIDE ~ CAULKED SEAMS
BOTTOM PLANKING ~ 1⅛" W OAK OR W CEDAR
    LAID ATHWARTSHIP ~ 5½" WIDE PLANKS ~
    CAULKED SEAMS
DECK BEAMS ~ 1" × 2¼" SPRUCE; EXCEPT BEAMS
    AT MAST BENCH TO BE 1⅛" × 2¼" W OAK
DECK ~ 1⅛" W CEDAR
CARLINGS ~ 1⅛" × 2½" SPRUCE
CLAMP ~ ⅞" × 3¾" FIR, TAPER ENDS
GROUNDING STRIPS ~ 1¼" × 2½" W OAK
TRANSOM ~ 1¼" W OAK, 5 PLANKS, FRAMED
    WITH 1¼" × 3½" W OAK
SKEG ~ 1½" W OAK

RAISED DECK
SIDE FRAMES ~ ¾" × 2¼" SPRUCE
SIDES ~ ¾" W CEDAR
FASHION PIECE ~ 1¼" × 3¾" W OAK (SEE DETAIL)
BATTEN ~ 1" × 3" FIR
TOP BEAMS ~ ¾" × 2¼" SPRUCE, 11" C TO C
TOP ~ ⅜₆" T & G W CEDAR, CANVAS
    COVERED (8 OZ)
AFT END OF RAISED DECK ~ ¾" × 4" W CEDAR
    T & G
CENTERBOARD & TRUNK
C'BOARD ~ 1¼" W OAK, DOWEL WITH ⅜" GALV ROD
HEAD LEDGES ~ 1⁹⁄₁₆" W OAK
BED LOGS ~ 1¾" × 6" W OAK
TRUNK SIDES ~ 1⅛" W OAK
TRIM
RAIL ~ 1⅜" × 2¾" W OAK (SEE DETAIL)
SHEER MOLDING ~ 1¾" D HR W OAK
COCKPIT COAMING ~ ⅜" × 4" W OAK
MOLDING TOP OF RAISED DECK ~ ¾" D HR
    W OAK

Construction drawings of Shore Liner. *The complete working drawings in-clude a plywood construction section.*

John Bete's Up Beat *lying at her mooring in Marion, Massachusetts. John and his brother built* Up Beat *and* Down Beat *from the design of* Shore Liner. *Approximately 60 of these shoal-draft centerboarders have been built.*

is arranged to slide under the cockpit deck when not in use, while a countertop is available to starboard. A water closet, not totally in conformity with today's regulations, consists of an enameled bucket tucked under the counter when not in use.

The cockpit seats are flush with the deck and may be used for sleeping during particularly warm weather. The cockpit floor extends out from the cabin, but its run is interrupted by a high sill designed to prevent water from entering the cabin.

The deck arrangement is practical and simple; nothing projects to catch sheets and other rigging. The raised sides and deck amidship increase the space below, and with its tumblehome, this superstructure is well adapted to the design.

The sail plan is very simple and features a total area of 363 square feet: 215 square feet in the mainsail and 148 in the staysail. The deep reefs indicated were requested by Ed Hanks. These will prove of value many times over.

Lazyjacks are rigged on the main boom and the staysail club. The mast is set in a tabernacle to enable the owner to lower the mast for the exploration of shallow creeks, which are often bridged over.

Some time after the design of *Shore Liner* was published, I prepared a double-headsail rig for A.R. Dussinger, of Springfield, Massachusetts. This provided additional sail area and worked out to advantage.

The construction and scantlings of *Shore Liner* are much the same as those of *New Sister* (see next chapter). Her working drawings also include a plywood construction section indicating the raised deck.

4

— New Sister —

24-foot flat-bottomed gaff-headed sloop

In this chapter are the sail plan, deck layout, cabin arrangement, elevation, and lines of an engaging little flat-bottomed auxiliary sloop. My father and I designed *New Sister* for F.S. (''Sky'') Wardwell of Glenbrook, Connecticut.

Taken with the 24-foot sloop *Shore Liner,* Wardwell asked us to design a boat of similar characteristics but one that incorporated a number of other, worthwhile features. Among these are the clipper bow and gaff-headed sail plan. Further, he asked us to draw up a trunk cabinhouse in place of the raised deck shown on *Shore Liner*'s plans.

The design was specially prepared for the amateur builder, and the boat, therefore, is of the utmost simplicity in hull form, construction, and rig. Wardwell built her following traditional standards, as outlined, while his brother Bob built a sistership using marine plywood. Thus, the working drawings include a construction section indicating this material.

It is worthy of note that the bottom is flat and the topsides straight from chine to deck edge. In consequence, these surfaces will be easy to plank with a minimum of labor and materials.

The dimensions of the sloop are 24 feet 3 inches overall by 21 feet 6

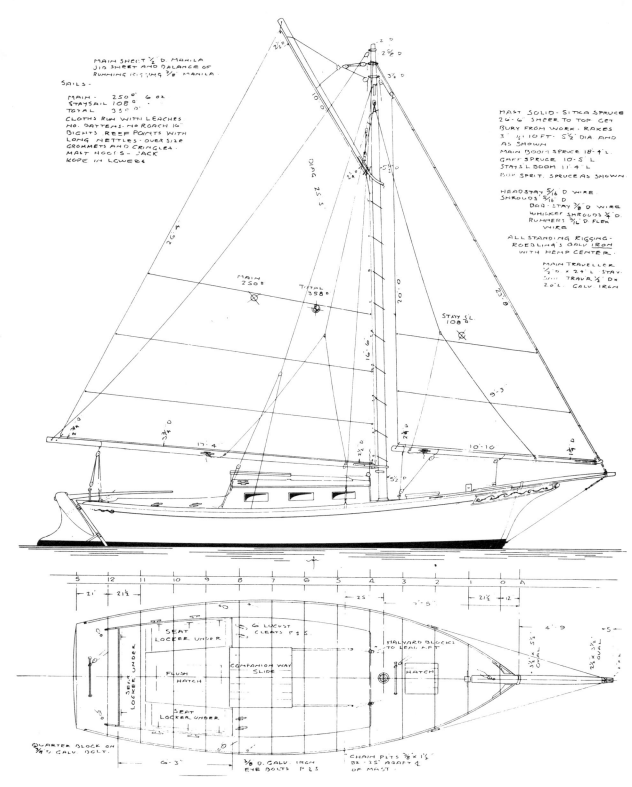

MAIN SHEET ½ D. MANILA
JIB SHEET AND BALANCE OF
RUNNING RIGGING ⅜ MANILA.

SAILS -

MAIN - 250□ 6 OZ
STAYSAIL 108□
TOTAL 358□
CLOTHS RUN WITH LEACHES
NO. BATTENS. NO ROACH 16"
BIGHTS REEF POINTS WITH
LONG NETTLES. OVER SIZE
GROMMETS AND CRINGLES.
MAST HOOPS - JACK
ROPE IN LOWERS

MAST SOLID - SITKA SPRUCE
26'-6" SHEER TO TOP. GET
BURY FROM WORK. RAKES
3". 4'-10 FT. 5½" DIA AND
AS SHOWN
MAIN BOOM SPRUCE 18'-4" L.
GAFF SPRUCE 10'-5" L.
STAYS'L BOOM 11'-4" L
BOW SPRIT. SPRUCE AS SHOWN.

HEADSTAY 5/16 D WIRE
SHROUDS 5/16 D
      DBN. STAY ⅜ D WIRE
      WHISKER SHROUDS ¼ D.
      RUNNERS 3/16 D FLEX
      WIRE

ALL STANDING RIGGING -
ROEBLING'S GALV IRON
WITH HEMP CENTER.

MAIN TRAVELLER
½ D x 29" L. STAY.
S'IL TRAV'R ½ D x
20" L. GALV. IRON

MAIN
250□

TOTAL
358□

STAY S'L
108□

QUARTER BLOCK ON
⅜ D GALV. BOLT.

SEAT
LOCKER UNDER

LOCKER UNDER

6 LOCUST
CLEATS P. & S.

COMPANION WAY
SLIDE

FLUSH
HATCH

SEAT
LOCKER UNDER

HALYARD BLOCKS
TO LEAD AFT

HATCH

⅜ D. GALV. IRON
EYE BOLTS P. & S.

CHAIN PLTS ⅜ x 1½"
BZ. 25" ABAFT ₵
OF MAST.

Despite her flat bottom and very shoal draft, New Sister is a cruising skiff that has proved handy and sea-worthy. Her gaff rig helps keep the sail plan low and safe.

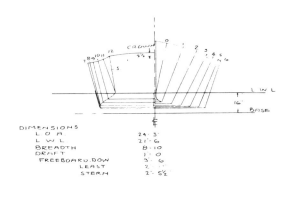

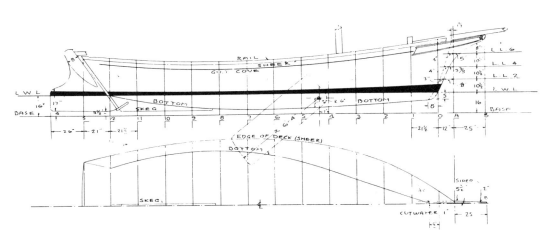

The lines of New Sister *indicate a time-proven flat-bottomed form. Notice the hollowness forward in her chine.*

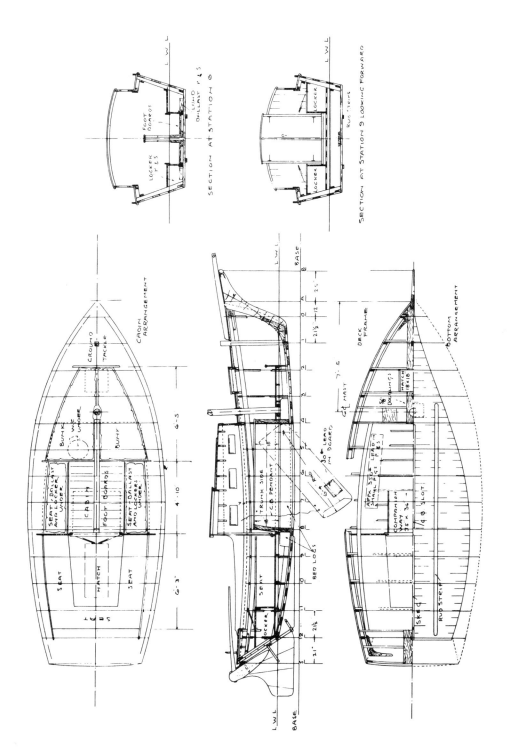

The deck arrangement, cabin plan, and construction profile show how New Sister utilizes every bit of space in her 24-foot length.

New Sister *on a close reach — off for Block Island. Sky Wardwell is at the helm, accompanied by his wife, Yvonne, for a weekend of relaxation. (Barlow photo)*

inches on her waterline. She has a beam of 8 feet 10 inches and a draft of 1 foot. The deepest part of the rudder also draws 1 foot of water.

The construction of the hull is on the heavy side, in keeping with strength, long life, and low upkeep. The specifications include: topsides, 1⅛ inches, white cedar; bottom planking, 1¾ inches, white cedar; side frames, 1¼ inches by 3 inches, white oak; keelson, 1¼ inches by 10 inches, white oak; deck beams, 1½ inches by 2¼ inches, spruce; and deck, ¾ inch by 3 inches, larch, white cedar, or other light wood.

Her cabin will accommodate two comfortably. The headroom beneath the cabintop beams is 4 feet 5 inches, and that under the companionway slide is 5 feet. The slide opening measures 3 feet square. A snug double berth is located forward; it is 6 feet 5 inches long and wide enough to guarantee two people uncrowded sleep.

Space beneath the after end of the berth allows for a fixed water-closet installation. The after end of the cabin itself has two fixed seats measuring 4 feet 10 inches long and featuring ample width for comfort.

The drawings show a large cockpit with seats running along either side as well as athwartships. All of these are fitted with hinged covers and provide excellent stowage space. The after seat is large enough to use for stowing an outboard engine, which will want to be of about 6 h.p.

New Sister carries a gaff-headed mainsail and a single jib. The total sail area in these is 350 square feet: 250 square feet in the main and 100 square feet in the staysail. The mast is solid and measures only 26 feet 6 inches from the deck to its truck. The standing rigging is simplicity itself — a single shroud each side, a headstay, runners, a bobstay and whisker shrouds.

Both Sky and Bob Wardwell report the sisters to be moderately fast, very stiff, comfortable, and fun to sail. This is a family boat that will give the most for the money invested to build her.

5

—— Tri Trainer ——

10-foot 10-inch flat-bottomed sailing skiff

A gentleman named Tom Hutson, formerly of Westport, Connecticut, conceived the *Tri Trainer*. He was very much involved in the City of Nor- walk's Youth Sailing Program, in which adults supervised youngsters in the process of learning the elements of small boat handling and sailing.

Hutson felt that the right boat would be one that could be used for training youngsters how to sail and row, and how to handle a small boat urged along by an outboard engine of modest power. It was also assumed that the boats might be built by various parents and their children, work- ing together as a learning experience. In response to Hutson's idea and requirements, I prepared the working drawings of *Tri Trainer*.

Tri Trainer's principal dimensions are 10 feet 10 inches overall by 10 feet on her waterline. She has a breadth of 4 feet 6½ inches and a draft of only 6 inches with the board up. Freeboard forward is 1 foot 9¼ inches, with 1 foot 3 inches at the stern and an even 1 foot at the lowest point. She is a burdensome boat, quite capable of carrying three 80-pound youngsters or a crew of father and son in complete safety.

I was quite taken by the little boat. My friend William W. Holcombe, a most competent amateur boatbuilder living in Newtown, Connecticut, was good enough to build one of the *Tri Trainers* for me, and we all enjoyed sailing her on Great Salt Pond, or New Harbor, at Block Island. She handled two of us ably and was very comfortable sailing along with Sailfish and other similar small boats on this lovely harbor.

Quite logically, the Hutson concept called for built-in flotation chambers port and starboard in the interest of safety for the youngsters. At my request, Bill Holcombe eliminated these, for I wanted simply to sit on the footboards and lean against the hull's side.

Jack Jacques, an excellent boatbuilder and the owner of the Dutch Wharf Yacht Yard, at Branford, Connecticut, built the spars and supplied the hardware for my *Tri Trainer* as a gesture of friendship and appreciation for "favors rendered" over the years. I redesigned the mainmast, which was made up of two lengths of fine Sitka spruce, neatly scarfed and joined in bronze ferrules.

I felt this was more practical than the original sliding gunter rig. The new mainmast stowed inboard when dismantled, as did the main boom. This made for easy trailering, and the loose-footed, jibheaded sail, made as a gift by my long-time friend Al Larsen of Port Washington, New York, set like a charm! Overall, my contribution to the boat was merely to provide the working drawings, for she was built and rigged by long-valued friends. She was a welcome gift!

The necessity of compromising in the development of any design is most interesting and proved to be so in the case of *Tri Trainer,* despite her modest dimensions and demands. In working out the boat's various features, it was necessary to accept as well as reject ideas of merit in the interest of simplicity and low cost. The initial form of *Tri Trainer* is a compromise. While I believe there is much to be said for flat-bottomed boats, there is also considerable merit in athwartships rocker, after the manner of the engaging and handsome Penguin-class dinghies.

Even in smaller hulls, the lifting qualities of such rocker — as well as generally improved sailing characteristics — are reasonably well established. A further advantage is the increase in the strength and stiffness of the underbody due to the slightly curved surface. However, the incorporation of this feature creates additional work for the more or less uninitiated builder; thus, a compromise was made in the interest of simplicity.

As shown, *Tri Trainer* carries a daggerboard, which is perfectly acceptable in many respects — particularly in a small boat. It is not as convenient or as practical as a pivoted centerboard, but on the other hand, it does not pose as much of a problem for the builder.

The hull is built from two 4-foot by 12-foot sheets of ¼-inch-thick waterproof fir or Philippine mahogany plywood. We used Bruynzeel

Sail plan and interior arrangement of the Tri Trainer. *The little boat is built of ¼-inch waterproof plywood. The flotation chambers outboard to port and starboard are formed by the main decks, longitudinal bulkheads, and hull topsides, which encase Styrofoam blocks cut to fill the voids.*

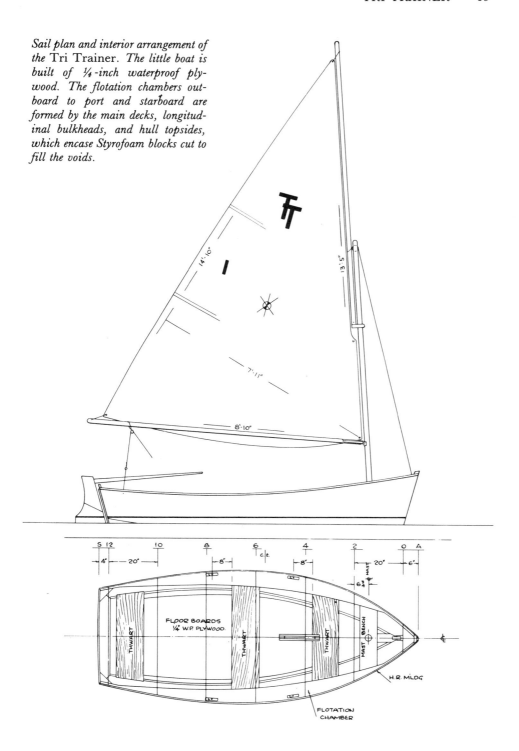

My shipmate, David Nielson, sailing Tri Trainer *in light air at New Harbor, Block Island, Rhode Island. In all little boats, live ballast plays a great role in trim. There is a clean run at her transom well free of the water, thus eliminating drag. The mainmast is arranged with a 12-inch scarf with the nib ends tucked into bronze ferrules. The standing rigging is kept taut by lashings at the lower ends. The mainsail is laced to the mast and the sail is loose-footed. Every effort has been made to maintain simplicity.*

rotary-cut mahogany ply, which proved to be excellent. The boat's bottom is gotten out of one sheet, her port and starboard sides from the other. Jib-ends and those irregularly shaped pieces remaining will do for chine gussets and other miscellaneous members.

One additional sheet of ¼-inch plywood, measuring 4 feet by 10 feet, will be required for her decks. It will also be needed for construction of the longitudinal flotation bulkhead if these chambers are incorporated. Ideally, they should be included if the little boat is to be used for training purposes.

Plywood was selected because of its tendency to remain tight, its ease of assembly, its strength, its relative lightness, and its availability. Glass tape, impregnated with resin, can be turned over her chine if there is any doubt about the tightness of this joint. If the components are put together adequately, however, there is no need for the tape.

I undertook an experiment with my boat, one that proved to be ill advised. I wanted to observe the ability of glass cloth to adhere to the plywood over an extended period of time, so I covered the entire exterior of the boat with 10-ounce glass cloth impregnated with epoxy resin. The cloth's weight, combined with that of the resin, increased the weight of the finished boat substantially — to the point of making her heavy to haul ashore — and decreased her ability to float when filled with water.

I also experienced problems in obtaining the proper paint to cover the epoxy: It proved difficult to obtain the high degree of finish I desired. If I were doing the job again, I would not cover the plywood with anything but a first-class, time-proven paint.

Tri Trainer's overall dimensions make her just a bit on the large side for use as a dinghy aboard the average cruiser or auxiliary. It is my feeling, however, that she had to be burdensome enough to be safe for her original purpose.

No complications should be experienced with her construction. Of course, it is advisable to redraw the hull full size from the lines and offsets to "get off on the right foot."

6

—— Erika ——

14-foot 9-inch flat-bottomed sailing skiff

Erika is a larger, slightly modified version of my father's highly successful sailing skiff *Dicky*. Concerning *Dicky,* he wrote, " . . . The trouble with about 95% of the flat-bottom boats built is that they are simply 'built,' little thought having been devoted to their ultimate shape . . . . When a builder works without well-thought-out designs, the boats turned out row hard, will not sail properly, and push hard under the power of an outboard engine."

Erika is 14 feet 9 inches long, 13 feet 9 inches on the waterline, and 4 feet 2½ inches in breadth. She has 3½ inches draft with the centerboard up. The freeboard at the bow is 1 foot 9 inches and at the stern 1 foot 4½ inches. *Erika* is designed to refute the notion that a flat-bottomed boat will always row hard and sail indifferently.

The bottom is much narrower than the deck, the topsides having generous flare. Any kind of skiff that is as wide on the bottom as it is on deck will have no reserve stability — thus it tends to be on the dangerous side. Generally speaking, the more flare in the topsides, the safer and better the boat will be. Unfortunately, you will find few skiffs of the latter kind — most are nearly slab-sided, more's the pity.

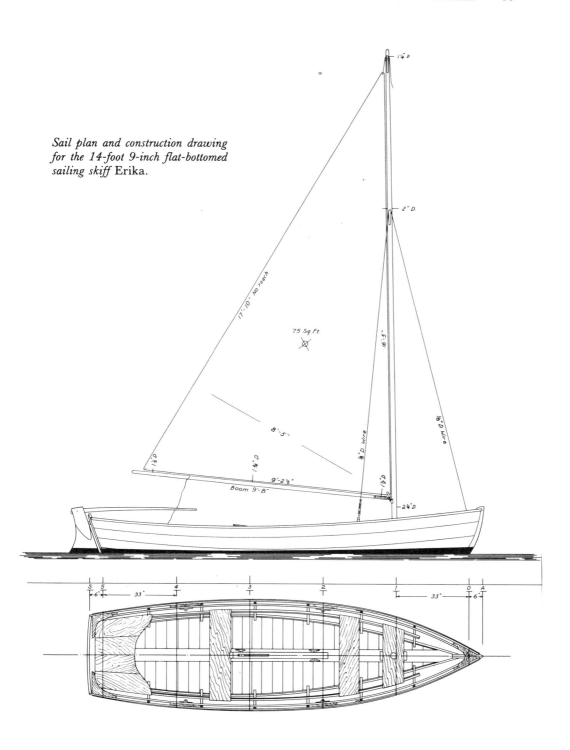

Sail plan and construction drawing for the 14-foot 9-inch flat-bottomed sailing skiff Erika.

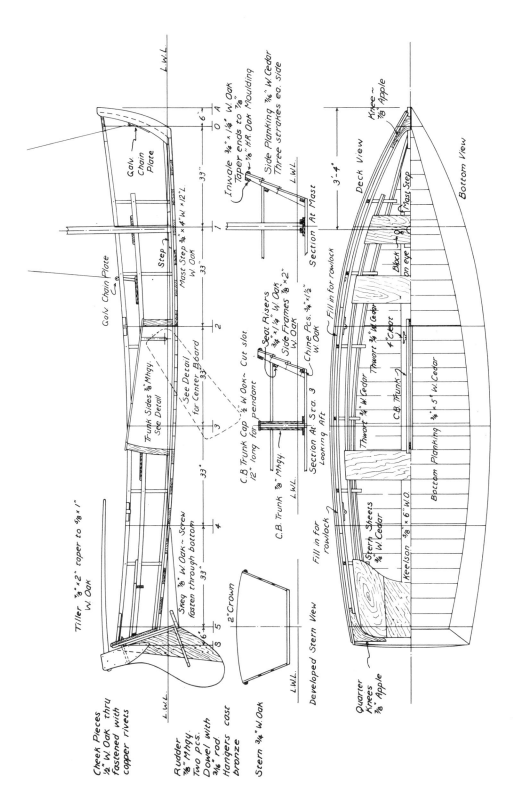

More construction drawings of Erika. The working drawings include details of her centerboard, centerboard trunk, and rudder.

The fore-and-aft sweep, or curve, of the bottom of *Erika* is a fair curve, not a straight line with a quick "turn-up" at its after end. Fair curves slide through the water more easily than humpy curves, and the more easily a boat passes through the water, the less power is needed to propel it. Reasonable sharpness of the waterline forward is another quality that helps the skiff progress through the water. This fineness also eases the tendency to pound that is common to all flat-bottomed boats — and this is particularly true when the boat is urged along by an outboard engine.

If *Erika* is to be used only for rowing — or with an outboard engine of modest power — it will not be necessary to install the centerboard or the rudder.

The sail plan is designed for handy sailing and for neophyte sailors. The area is 75 square feet. It is to be made of lightweight (3 ounces or less) Dacron sailcloth. Be sure to go to a good sailmaker for sails — which, after all, are power and therefore should be efficient if you expect good performance.

Erika could very well be built of ⅜-inch-thick marine plywood — which has the advantage of staying tight if the little boat will be left out of the water for extended periods.

7

—— Martha Green ——

24-foot skipjack powerboat

Bill Holcombe builds boats in Newtown, Connecticut. Over the past 25 years he has built, in his spare time, about 12 Atkin-designed boats — ranging from the 7-foot *Cabin Boy* to the 24-foot *Martha Green* shown here.

The scow *Sedge,* a houseboat *All Square,* and the fast V-bottomed *Josephine,* among others, have grown in the woodland boatshop of my friend. Bill finds a great deal of satisfaction in this rewarding hobby and he has become a competent, knowledgeable craftsman in the bargain.

The workmanship in each of his vessels surpasses its predecessor — and each is practical and straightforward and departs from the ordinary. *Martha Green* is the latest of the Holcombe fleet, and there is nothing *ordinary* about her.

Principal dimensions are 24 feet overall by 21 feet 6 inches on the waterline by 8 feet 4 inches beam and 2 feet 11 inches draft. She is a ''deadrise'' hull and was conceived as ''simple to build.''

Experience indicates once again that no boat is ''simple to build.'' All those worth their salt, by the very nature of being so, are complex — and all are well worth the time spent in their creation. However, *Martha Green* is a fundamentally simple boat — there is virtually constant deadrise and

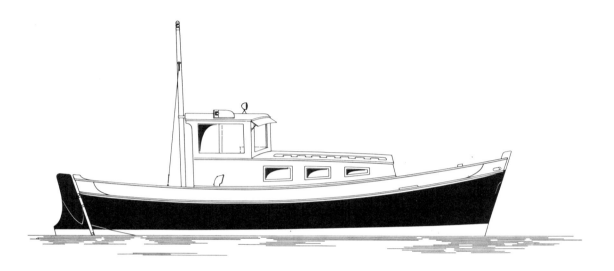

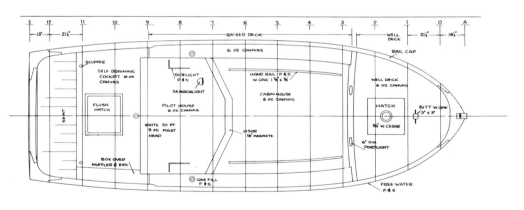

Profile and deck arrangement of the 24-foot Martha Green. *A 130-square-foot ketch steadying rig designed for E.W. Gibbons of Bermuda created an able motorsailer with the ability to run and reach — and to work to windward under the urging of the auxiliary engine. Thomas W.P. Vesey, also of Bermuda, ordered a sistership,* Lady of the Lake, *and she too proved most successful.*

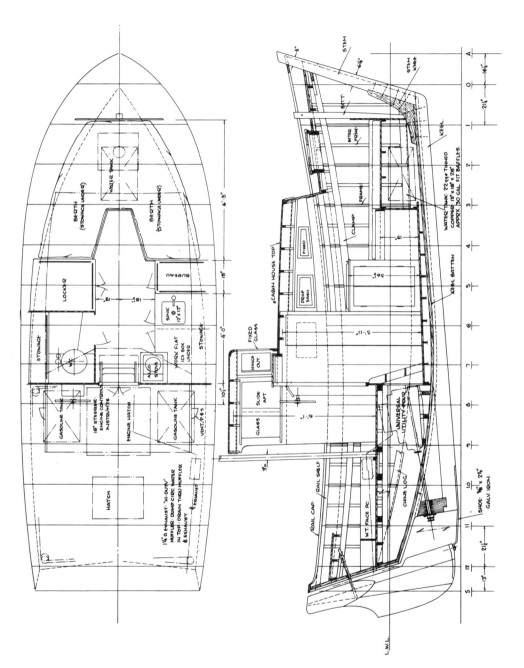

Construction and arrangement plans of Martha Green. Her galley is 4 feet long and the berths, forward, are 6 feet 3 inches. There is 5-foot 11-inch headroom under the trunk beams and 6 feet 1 inch under the standing top.

constant flare, with no flam introduced in her forward sections. Her forefoot is constructed after the fashion of the Chesapeake Bay skipjacks — staved up in a vertical manner for some 20 to 24 inches abaft the stem. At this point, bottom planking is laid diagonally about 45 degrees to the hull centerline.

Martha Green is powered by a Universal Utility Four fitted with a 2:1 reduction gear. With this little mill she slides along at a comfortable, and amazingly quiet, 9 to 10 m.p.h. And she is capable of maintaining this speed when the sea builds up.

Her arrangement plan indicates built-in berths in the forward part of the hull, with good sitting room in the aft portion of the berths. The galley, to starboard, is more than ample, with a bureau at its forward end, ash work surface, sink, and alcohol range. An icebox is fitted beneath the galley work surface. To port, a large shelf-top hanging locker provides excellent stowage for shore clothes. The enclosed toilet room is about 3 feet 6 inches long. There is 5-foot 11-inch headroom beneath the house-top beams.

The open cockpit, partially protected by a standing top or "pilothouse," is a delightful place to spend an afternoon on the sparkling waters inshore of our lovely Norwalk islands. A flush deck, fitted with adequate hatches, covers the power plant.

There appears to be continuing interest in wholesome little vessels of the nature of *Martha Green*. Over the years since she was designed, a great many of these boats have been built, including several in Bermuda. There is much to be said for the boat's relatively low initial cost, economy of operation, and minimum upkeep.

John Little, then at Old Lyme, Connecticut, built a sistership for a Doctor Chace of Middletown. This boat is now owned by the Davis family, and I see her each summer at Block Island. With all due respects, her black hull, white boottop, and white bulwark rails create a distinctive and attractive hooker.

THE BUILDER SPEAKS
by William W. Holcombe

Boats under 25 feet in length suffer from lack of room: headroom, foot room, and elbow room. Furthermore, they tend to be very active in a seaway, with quick motions that tire the crew and throw gear about the cabin and decks. In any kind of a sea beyond a mere chop, they are frequently hard to steer and often take solid water on deck.

The problem that I presented to John Atkin was not easily solved, since I asked him to design a hull that would, insofar as possible, eliminate all those difficulties.

I wanted a boat with easy motion, 6 feet of headroom in the cabin and under the standing top, berths wide enough and long enough to furnish reasonable sleeping comfort and ample foot room on the cabin sole. In addition to all that, I wanted a cockpit large enough for four people for day trips, a decent galley, an ample toilet room, and side decks wide enough to go forward upon with some hope of arriving.

Owning a boat of any size has become very expensive. When one adds the cost of building and storing to the rental of a slip, maintenance of the hull and house, and the replacement of gear, the total reaches a respectable sum. So, another requirement was an economical power plant: economical to maintain and inexpensive to buy. Too many boats today are grossly overpowered, and I wanted to avoid stepping into that trap. I also wanted to avoid paying for gasoline wasted in an over-large power plant that would do little but suck the stern down and drag a huge sea.

Not the least important consideration was a boat that looks like a boat. I am not an admirer of the modern streamlined cruiser with its acres of glass and square yards of chrome plating. Streamlining in most boats is unnecessary, and in a boat designed to go along slowly, it is merely silly. Furthermore, it adds to the cost of building in time, labor, and money.

Martha Green was built over a two-year period. In point of fact, the building took one year and 11 months from lofting to launching. Not all that time was spent in actual work, however. Since I kept no records of the time spent, I can only guess that it amounted to about 3,000 hours. Working alone on a project of this size is, for me at any rate, a slow business.

She was built in a 19th-century barn in the foothills of the Berkshires about 30 miles from her homeport on Long Island Sound. She was launched from a heavy trailer that carried her down in about four hours, including loading time.

I built the hull upside down, which made the bottom planking easier to do and also helped somewhat with the side planking. As soon as she was turned over, she was set on a cradle, which became the building stocks. The keel, stem, deadwood, and horn timber were assembled carefully on the shop floor and then set up to marks with the waterline level and everything plumb. The side frames were also made on the floor, with cross spalls at the waterline and sheer. They were then set up plumb and level, using the centerline and the waterline as reference points. The transom frame was made as a unit and set upon a jig erected in its proper place in relation to the backbone and the frames. The jig was made carefully from the loft drawings.

Planking the bottom was a simple process, as she is planked crosswise on a diagonal from the keel rabbet to the chine. All the planks are parallel-sided and are from 4 to 6 inches in width. The only difficult part of the bottom planking was closing in the 2 feet abaft the stem. Here the great twist required thick staving, which had to be dubbed to shape and thickness. This is in the tradition of some of the workboats on Chesapeake Bay. This part of the job could also have been done chunk-style, as in some of the Chesapeake oystermen. [The working drawings indicate large-scale alternate methods of building this area. — J.A.]

Due to the bold sheer, her topside planking presented a nice exercise in lining off. A good many stealers had to be worked in forward. This is not a particularly difficult process, but it had to be done carefully. The results were good, and the hull strength was maintained by placing the stealers between planks that run the full length of the hull and by generous use of carefully fitted butt blocks. In a hull of this type, the lining off must be well planned before the first plank is laid.

The keel, stem, deadwood, and horn timber are made of Thai teak. The rest of the hull — including frames, planking, chines, and clamps — is made of African mahogany. The bottom planking is a full 1¼ inches in thickness and the side planking is ⅝ inch. The house side staving is ¾-inch redwood, screw fastened. The cabin and the standing top beams are of eastern pine covered with mahogany plywood, canvased. The foredeck is tongue-and-groove fir, fiberglassed.

All the fastenings are Everdur bronze. The seams were caulked with cotton and stopped with rubber seam compound. All the deck hardware is bronze, and the special hardware is manganese bronze. I made all the patterns and did some of the machining, which saved a great deal of money and resulted in hardware specially adapted to the job.

The engine installed is a 4-91 Gray "Sea Scout" with a 2:1 Paragon gear turning a 19-inch-diameter by 13-inch-pitch Columbian wheel. This is enough power for the hull form. On her shakedown cruise she was timed carefully over long courses between fixed marks, and she averaged 8½ statute miles over the ground at 2,000 r.p.m., with a minimum of vibration and noise and a gasoline consumption of just under 1¾ gallons per hour.

A boat like this is not for everybody, but for me she has many advantages. She goes along without dragging a heavy sea, she rolls and pitches moderately and with an easy motion, and she does not pound. The 1,500 pounds of lead pigs that she requires to put her down to her designed waterline are stowed to dampen her rolling. With her 3 feet of draft, deep deadwood, and large rudder, she handles well in close quarters. In a following sea she shows no tendency to yaw widely and has never threatened to broach.

Bill Holcombe's Martha Green *is a practical powerboat. The 24-footer represents simplicity of construction yet provides a wholesome little vessel of unusual interest. Her relatively big, slow-turning propeller wheel, tucked well down in the water, is most effective. There is a flush deck over the engine.*

It is true that she is slow, but it seems to me that the pleasure to be found in small boats is in the going, not the arriving. If the going is pleasant, reasonably quiet, and quite comfortable, then the arriving is all the more satisfactory.

8

—Nina—

11-foot 4-inch flat-bottomed sailing skiff

There is a lot to be said for simplicity. *Nina* is a most practical and useful type of boat. Despite her modest dimensions — from her flat bottom to the tip of her unstayed mast — *Nina* is very much of a little ship.

She is an excellent craft in which to learn to sail — as well as to learn to become a seaman aware of the ways of wind and weather. She is a boat that will sail safely in rough, windy weather — in confidence and with lots of fun. When the wind is more than she can handle in safety and comfort, a small outboard engine will urge her along in good style. How much more practical it is for youngsters to learn the ways of the water in such a boat than to use a "skimming dish" rigged with hiking slings and all the complications of far too many of today's "youth training" boats used by yacht clubs.

Nina's dimensions are 11 feet 4 inches overall with a breadth of 4 feet 7 inches and 4½ inches of draft. *Nina* will carry a cargo of two heavy persons nicely, or three average-size youngsters. Possibly among the best of her features is the fact that she can be built by an amateur or professional boatbuilder for a modest amount of money. Quarter-inch waterproof plywood can be used for her underbody and topsides, as is true of many of the flat-bottomed hulls shown in this book.

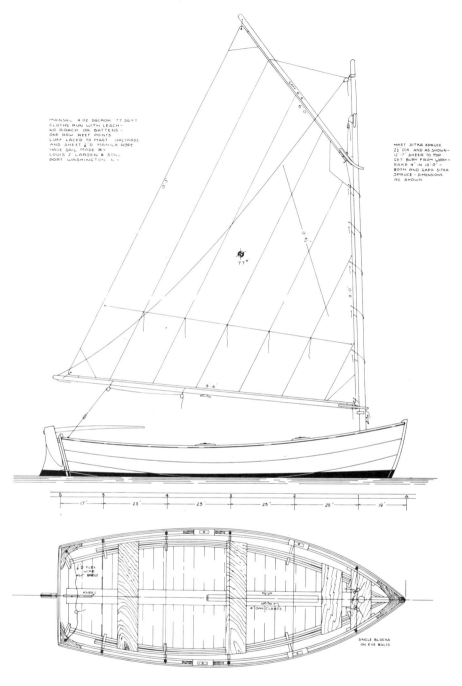

MAINSAIL 4 OZ DACRON 77 SQ FT
CLOTHS RUN WITH LEACH -
NO ROACH OR BATTENS -
ONE ROW REEF POINTS
LUFF LACED TO MAST HALYARDS
AND SHEET ½ D MANILA ROPE
HAVE SAIL MADE BY
LOUIS J LARSEN & SONS
PORT WASHINGTON, N Y

MAST SITKA SPRUCE
2¼ DIA AND AS SHOWN -
12'-7" SHEER TO TOP -
GET BURY FROM WORK -
RAKE 4" IN 10'-0" -
BOOM AND GAFF SITKA
SPRUCE - DIMENSIONS
AS SHOWN

The Nina's *gaff rig suits the simplicity of the hull. Although* Nina *is ideally suited to sailing, she will row nicely. Should the wind peter out, she can be urged home by an "ash breeze."*

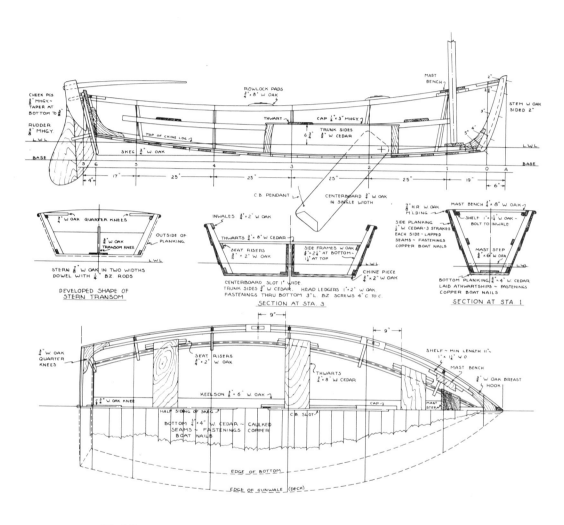

The Nina *belongs to a respected lineage of similar flat-bottomed boats. Her construction follows traditional standards.*

The station molds, or forms, of Nina *set up at Charles McNeil's shop in Morehead City, North Carolina. Two by fours are leveled on the earth to provide a building stage. While a wood or concrete floor would be more ideal, the ingenious builder is able to overcome many obstacles. The station molds and cross spalls, made of a relatively poor grade of pine, are more than satisfactory for the purpose. These are braced securely to ensure alignment. A string is stretched taut from the forward perpendicular to a similar member aft to provide a reference for measuring.*

Charles McNeil's Nina *is shown with her topsides planked. Her stem has been rabbeted to accommodate the hood ends of the planks. Rabbets cut in the forward opposing edges of the planks allow them to fit flush with the side of the stem. The keelson, or keel batten, is notched into the station molds and her bottom is about ready to be fitted.*

The 11-foot 4-inch rowing version of Nina *with her skipper rowing and the "crew" keeping an eye out for boardings. Charles McNeil used waterproof plywood for the little boat's bottom.*

Nina *running before a light summer breeze and displaying the burdensome quality and simplicity of the flat-bottomed boat.*

Dimensions for making the forms are indicated on the lines drawing. From these dimensions, redraw the lines full size on a convenient surface — Upson board, or heavy building paper, would be practical. It is necessary to "loft" — or redraw — the lines to determine the location of the stem, the depth and bevel of the stem rabbet, and bevels on the frames in the event she is built of plywood and side frames stand vertically and athwartship frames are installed.

Her single sail should be about 4-ounce Dacron. One of the Howe and Bainbridge colored fabrics — such as their tanbark — would look attractive with the topsides painted white and the interior a nice mast buff. What a handsome little vessel she will be!

9

—— Florence Oakland ——

22-foot 5-inch V-bottomed schooner

In this age of "efficiency," it is encouraging to see the continuing interest in the likes of my little gaff-headed schooner *Florence Oakland*. There are genuine yachtsmen the world over who maintain great love for "little ships of tradition and worth." One such person, Jacob Hess, of Canton, Ohio, wrote me some time ago and outlined his thoughts about a little boat that could be sailed near her home on Lake Atwood, Ohio, and trailed easily, so that Jake, his wife, Furf, and their two girls could drive east to Oyster Bay where she could try her wings on Long Island Sound or farther down east.

Jake wrote, "For some time we have considered having designed and built a traditional daysailer for use on our small Ohio lakes and on Long Island Sound. We shall call our new little ship *Florence Oakland,* the maiden name of my wife's mother. The enclosed sketch is a general representation of some of our ideas."

With this introduction and his accompanying sketch, I prepared a scale preliminary study of the proposed yacht's profile (sail plan) and arrangement and sent it to him. He replied, "We are delighted with the preliminary of the little schooner! She is a splendid ship."

In the months that followed, I prepared the working drawings. *Florence Oakland* is a V-bottomed hull 22 feet 5 inches overall by 20 feet on the waterline by 7 feet 8 inches beam by 3 feet of draft. I showed a long, fairly shallow lead casting weighing 1,200 pounds for outside ballast and 300 pounds of inside lead, after the manner of proper little cruising boats where comfort is considered before yacht racing rules.

Florence Oakland has modest drag to her keel and an ample outboard rudder. I gave the hull what I thought to be proper deadrise and ample flare to her topsides, continuing this aft until introducing a bit of "shape" above the chine to avoid the appearance of boxiness to her transom.

Although Jake and I agreed with the late L. Francis Herreshoff that conventional planking is better, we decided on marine plywood because the little ship was to be trailer-borne from time to time, and we wanted her to stay tight. So, her lines were developed accordingly. (A young boatbuilder named Paul Gartside in Cornwall, England, built a sistership utilizing conventional batten seam construction.)

It is particularly rewarding to develop the lines of a small boat. I suspect it's the most interesting of all the tasks involved in preparing a complete design. One must see that the ends bear a relationship to one another, that the sheer is "active," the waterline balanced, that a handsome vessel results from the long hours of fiddling with splines and curves, that a successful boat results (based, in my case, on the performance of a great many predecessors). Thanks to Maynard Lowery of Tilghman Island, Maryland, who faithfully and expertly followed my working drawings in building *Florence Oakland,* the little schooner was launched and tried successfully on the Chesapeake.

In a letter sometime later, Jake Hess provided me with a report on the little boat's performance. He wrote, "Your little jewel has exceeded our requirements and expectations. She has been completely successful. She tacks in about 100 degrees and balances nicely on all points. On one long close reach from Tilghman to Oxford, I set the sails, lashed the helm, and spent most of the next half hour on the foredeck without touching helm or sheets.

"On a reach in moderate to planing winds she keeps up nicely with many of our local light-displacement boats, and on the Bay we held off a fiberglass 'something or other' for an entire morning. She is a beauty and much admired by all who have seen her. The whole concept of something so unusual as a schooner on our lake has been enthusiastically accepted."

Sails for *Florence Oakland* were made by Al Larsen, at Port Washington, New York, and these set beautifully. The blocks, deadeyes, cleats, belaying pins, mast hoops, and hardware are from A. Dauphinee & Sons, Lunenburg, Nova Scotia.

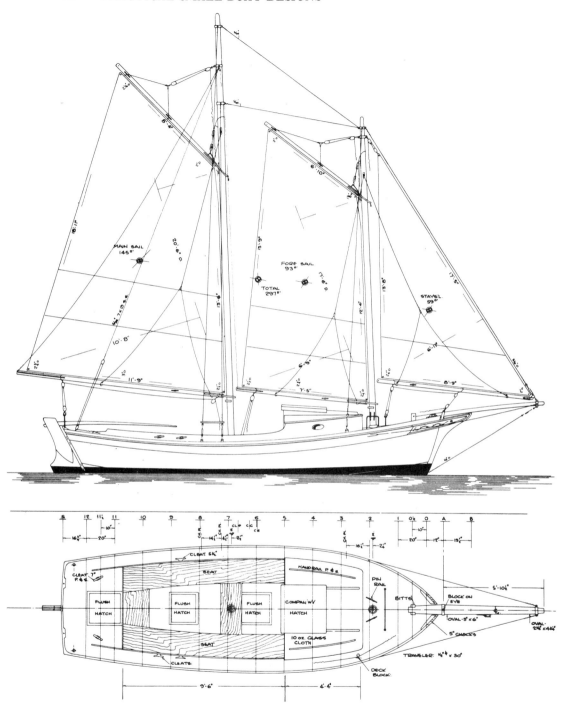

The sail plan of Florence Oakland, *including her deck arrangement plan. She handles nicely, much like a little ship. Not conceived for offshore work, she is entirely capable in waters such as those of Long Island Sound.*

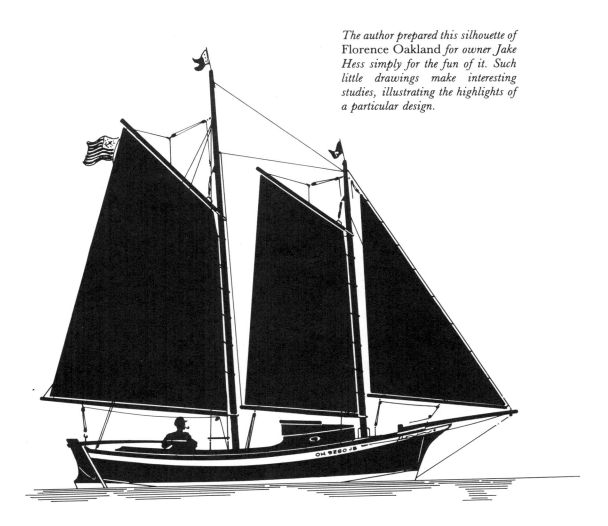

The author prepared this silhouette of
Florence Oakland *for owner Jake Hess simply for the fun of it. Such little drawings make interesting studies, illustrating the highlights of a particular design.*

The arrangement plan and elevation show two berths in addition to a small locker on each side in the cuddy. The ample cockpit can accommodate four comfortably. An outboard engine, installed in a well, provides auxiliary power.

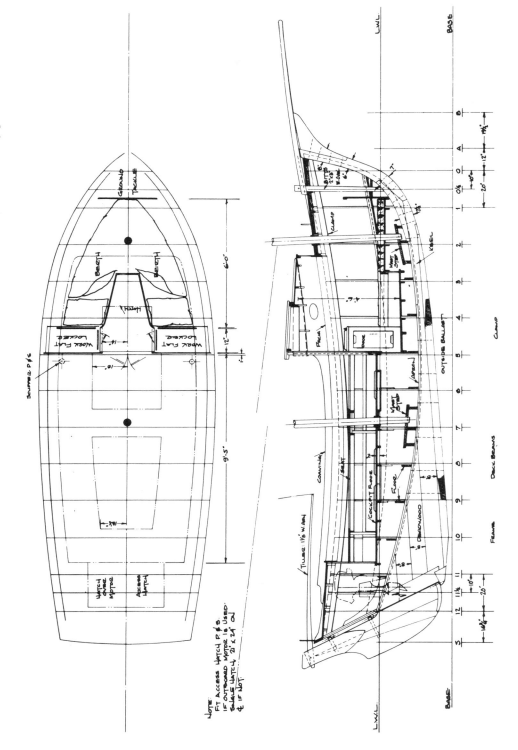

Sifting along on a broad reach, Florence Oakland *represents ''a true little ship.'' She balances beautifully with a minimum of fuss around the rudder, demanding but one hand on the tiller.*

As of 1982, some 75 of the little schooners had been built by both professional and amateur builders worldwide. Irving D. Giese of Ascona, Switzerland — who has built many boats from designs by my father and me — undertook the construction of *Florence Oakland,* and she is sailed on Lake Maggiore, which is a long, relatively narrow body of water extending between northern Italy and Switzerland. We have sailed there, with Irving and his friends Carlino and Ninon, on one of my father's *Little Maid of Kent* schooners. This was a memorable occasion, and the afternoon sail was climaxed by a visit to a shoreside grotto, where my wife and I thoroughly enjoyed drinking wine in the company of Irving and his friends. It was a special day that will continue to be with us for years to come.

Jake Hess's original little schooner was destroyed by fire. He telephoned me, deeply concerned about the prospects of duplicating her.

Maynard Lowery said he would have had to increase the price substantially — considerably more than Jake's insured valuation. We shopped around and found that John Little, then building boats in Old Lyme, Connecticut, was in a position to undertake the work. John did a first-class job in all respects and duplicated the original without a change. Jake has told me that the ''new'' boat is behaving quite up to her earlier sister.

10

—— Valgerda* ——

18-foot 7-inch Hardangersjekte

My friend Jon Wilson, publisher of *WoodenBoat* magazine, has always been very interested in the design of *Valgerda*. He asked me to assemble her drawings for publication in *WoodenBoat*, and the design appeared in the January/February 1979 issue of that grand magazine.

This type of boat originated in the Hardangerfjord, Norway — thus she is a Hardangersjekte, ''jekte'' meaning boat. The first one I remember seeing was on the South Shore of Long Island. My father and I were driving along the busy Merrick Road and we saw her at a sales agency. She stood out among a fleet of mundane flat- and V-bottomed outboard boats. Later my shipmates Bjarne Neilson and his partner, Ed Weber, who operated Norge Boats in Darien, Connecticut, imported one of the boats for R.E. Condon of Valley Forge, Pennsylvania. While she was at Norge, I was able to take off her lines. She is very close, indeed, to the original Hardangersjekte.

In their homeland the boats are used for fishing and other practical work. They were designed for rowing, but many of the boats now are rigged with a tall, narrow sail plan — with hollow spars and light standing rigging.

The design of Valgerda is published with permission of Hearst Marine Books, New York.

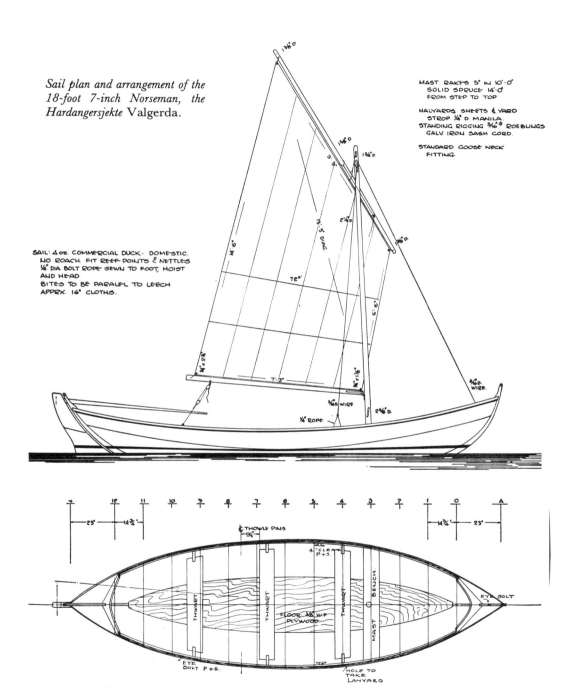

Sail plan and arrangement of the 18-foot 7-inch Norseman, the Hardangersjekte Valgerda.

MAST RAKES 5" IN 10'·0"
SOLID SPRUCE 14'·0"
FROM STEP TO TOP

HALYARDS SHEETS & YARD
STROP ¼" D. MANILA.
STANDING RIGGING ³/₁₆"∅ ROEBLINGS
GALV. IRON SASH CORD.

STANDARD GOOSE NECK
FITTING.

SAIL: 4 OZ. COMMERCIAL DUCK. DOMESTIC.
NO ROACH. FIT REEF POINTS & NETTLES
¼" DIA. BOLT ROPE SEWN TO FOOT, HOIST
AND HEAD.
BITES TO BE PARALEL TO LEECH
APPRX. 16" CLOTHS.

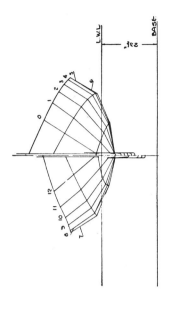

The lines drawings of Valgerda.

SHEER (EDGE OF WALE)

CHINE #1

CHINE #2

KEEL

LEAD · 2" T × 3" H × 42" L.

RABBET

STEM SIDED 1⅛"

SHEER (EDGE OF WALE)

CHINE #1

CHINE #2

HALF SIDING OF KEEL

L.W.L

BASE

L.W.L

BASE

Deck and bottom construction plans of Valgerda, *with section 7 and rudder-tiller plan.*

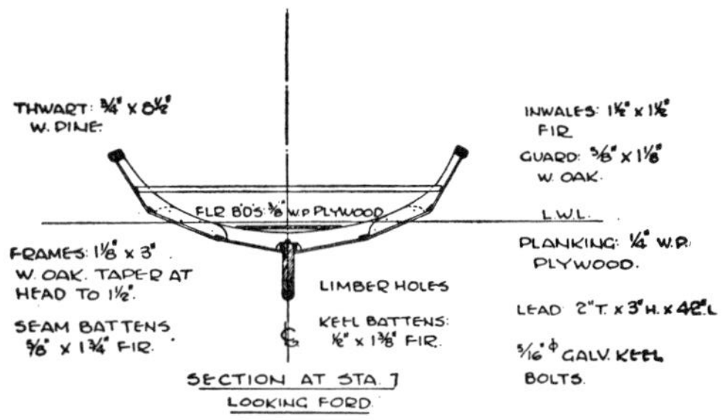
THWART: 3/4" x 8 1/2" W. PINE
FIR B'D'S 3/8" W.P. PLYWOOD
L.W.L.
FRAMES: 1 1/8" x 3" W. OAK. TAPER AT HEAD TO 1 1/2".
SEAM BATTENS 3/8" x 1 3/4" FIR.
LIMBER HOLES
KEEL BATTENS: 1/2" x 1 3/8" FIR.
INWALES: 1 1/2" x 1 1/2" FIR
GUARD: 3/8" x 1 1/8" W. OAK.
PLANKING: 1/4" W.P. PLYWOOD.
LEAD 2" T. x 3" H. x 42" L
5/16" ϕ GALV. KEEL BOLTS.
SECTION AT STA. 7
LOOKING FORD

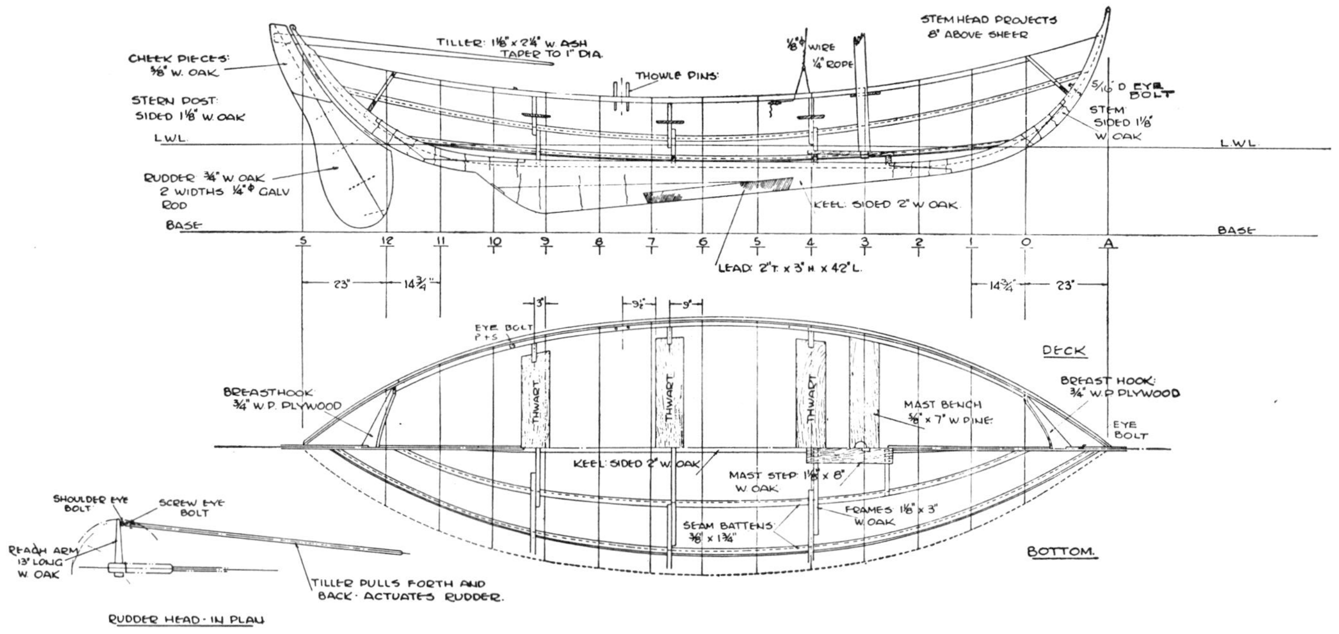
CHEEK PIECES: 3/8" W. OAK
STERN POST: SIDED 1 1/8" W. OAK
L.W.L.
RUDDER 3/4" W. OAK 2 WIDTHS 1/4" ϕ GALV ROD
BASE
TILLER: 1 1/8" x 2 1/4" W. ASH TAPER TO 1" DIA.
THOWLE PINS
1/8" ϕ WIRE
1/4" ROPE
STEM HEAD PROJECTS 8" ABOVE SHEER
5/16" D EYE BOLT
STEM SIDED 1 1/8" W. OAK
L.W.L.
KEEL: SIDED 2" W. OAK.
BASE
5 12 11 10 9 8 7 6 5 4 3 2 1 0 A
LEAD: 2" T. x 3" H x 42" L.
23"
14 3/4"
14 3/4"
23"
3"
9 1/2"
9"
EYE BOLT P+S
DECK
BREASTHOOK 3/4" W.P. PLYWOOD
THWART
THWART
THWART
MAST BENCH 3/8" x 7" W. PINE
BREAST HOOK: 3/4" W.P. PLYWOOD
EYE BOLT
KEEL SIDED 2" W. OAK
MAST STEP 1 1/8" x 8" W. OAK
FRAMES 1 1/8" x 3" W. OAK
SEAM BATTENS 3/8" x 1 3/4"
BOTTOM.
SHOULDER EYE BOLT
SCREW EYE BOLT
REACH ARM 13" LONG W. OAK
TILLER PULLS FORTH AND BACK · ACTUATES RUDDER.
RUDDER HEAD · IN PLAN

The "working boats" were fitted with an old-fashioned standing lug — and they depended for stability on a cargo of fish. Because of their lack of initial stability, I designed a new keel — the original boats had a long, shallow keel approximately 4 inches deep. When loaded, they had sufficient lateral plane to hold the little craft on the wind. With expert handling, they had little difficulty in reaching port. In many respects, the Hardangersjekte has the same basic characteristics as our Bank dory, the Maine peapod, and similar workboats. Present-day Coast Guard loading rules would not give the Hardangersjekte a very good rating, but they have tremendous reserve stability and are excellent sea boats.

Valgerda is 18 feet 7 inches overall by 14 feet 9 inches on her waterline by 5 feet 8 inches draft. Freeboard at her bow is 2 feet 6⅜ inches and 2 feet ½ inch at the stern.

She might very well be called a "double-chine" hull, which describes the sectional form very well; she will not be difficult to build. I have estimated that the finished boat will weigh about 600 pounds.

I've shown the standing lug rig — solid spruce mast, yard, and boom. Sail area is 72 square feet, which will be sufficient to reach and run as well as to work to windward after a fashion. I'm fond of the simplicity of the standing lug rig, and I feel that in a boat of this type, a low aspect ratio is more effective. I prepared the rather shoal fin keel, fitted with lead ballast of approximately 106 pounds, because of her lack of initial stability and the unlikelihood of her carrying a cargo of fish.

Her original construction incorporated ½-inch Scandinavian pine — laid in three strakes, which would require planks some 20 inches wide. Obviously this would be difficult, indeed, to come by! As a result, I've shown her planked with ¼-inch plywood, Harborite or Bruynzeel mahogany — both of which are excellent. The planks need not be in single lengths — and butt blocks may be used. The sheerstrake can be butted about amidships, the garboard at station 8, and the middle strake approximately halfway between stations 3 and 4. Butt blocks should be made of ¼-inch plywood about 8 inches long. Fastenings should be copper rivets. Between the laps, I would use one of the modern synthetic bedding compounds — ideally, one that does not set up too quickly. While originally faying surfaces were laid bare, the use of plywood will make the bedding material desirable. The breasthooks, or canted knees, bow and stern, can be made of ¾-inch Bruynzeel plywood — or laminated of white oak. These days it is very hard to find natural crooks.

A comprehensive "how-to-build" article about *Valgerda,* written by my father, is available along with working drawings, including her lines; table of offsets; construction plan, elevation, and sections; sail plan and interior arrangement plans. Scantlings are lettered on the drawings.

11

—— Great Bear ——

28-foot flat-bottomed sloop

Every morning I drink a toast, with my coffee, to my late friend Bill Dunn, who lived in Collingswood, New Jersey. It is rewarding to have known Bill — he was a special man, a special shipmate. Each summer my wife, Pat, and I would journey to Forked River, New Jersey, to spend a long weekend with our friend and to cruise on the Barnegat aboard one of the numerous Atkin-designed boats he owned over many years. Bill has sailed off to Valhalla and we savor our memories of him.

Bill Dunn was not an ordinary man; his tastes in yachts, for example, were unusual. Perhaps this is why our friendship was such a sound one. I, too, take a dim view of today's commonplace yachts — ones owned, no doubt, by the typical corporate-committee-oriented chap lacking in anything approaching originality.

I recall such a fellow who owned one of the many production yachts. He asked me to come aboard to see the unique setup that he had devised for rigging his club's pennant masthead staff. It was the only "unique" feature aboard the yacht — and that includes the owner! Surprisingly, his father was a prominent research chemist and a most entertaining gentleman. I well recall that he had his pet cat stuffed when it died, and it lay on the kitchen counter. I wonder where the individualism went?

But this is getting too far afield of Bill Dunn and his unusual shoal-draft sloop *Great Bear*. Her principal dimensions are 28 feet 10 inches overall by 26 feet on her waterline by 8 feet 7 inches beam. She has 1 foot 8 inches of draft with the board up. There is a total of 379.5 square feet of sail area — 282.5 square feet in the gaff main and 97 square feet in the roller-furling jib.

Great Bear has the distinction of being the "flagship" of this book of Atkin designs.

The 28-footer was built by Clement ("Pappy") Troth down in Tuckahoe, New Jersey. "Pappy" built all of Bill's boats, including his last one, a 36-foot "powerboat with sails," which I designed in 1965. There was some discussion in the Dunn family to the effect that the sloop should have window boxes beneath her rectangular windows and be named *Geranium,* but Bill took a dim view of that. Besides, he was fond of bears.

The *National Fisherman* featured *Great Bear* about 20 years ago, and they included the following description that I wrote of the boat. "The sloop might be termed a 'minimum gunkholer,' as she is of modest cost and shoal draft. The design was based on that of the flat-bottomed sloop *Twilight* designed by my father. In his quest for a simple, straightforward, and inexpensive design, Bill Dunn included *Twilight* among other possibilities.

"Reaching the conclusion that *Twilight* came close to meeting his needs but wanting slightly more in the manner of accommodations, as well as the desirable company of a suitable heating stove, the enlarged *Great Bear* was developed. Her arrangement plan indicates an enclosed toilet room to starboard. It is shut off, in part, from the engine compartment by the centerboard trunk — yet accessible from the main cabin by ducking beneath the midship bridge deck, as well as through the companionway.

"An ample galley area, including sink, ice chest, and two-burner stove, is shown to starboard in the main cuddy house — the stove stored under the main deck and fitted on proper slides for access when needed. Thirty gallons of gasoline are stowed in a low tank beneath the galley workflat, with room for stowage atop this. Opposite is the desired heating stove, a Fatsco Buddy wood-burning unit of economical first cost.

"The gaff rig is in keeping with the balance of the design and provides reasonable area with a low aspect ratio — an element worthy of consideration in handling a shoal-draft hull in safety and comfort.

"It must be kept in mind that this little vessel is a 'fun' boat — not intended for a party of six and all the glorious trappings abounding and felt essential in today's wonderful glittering world of boats. Nor is she intended to reach the windward mark some few seconds ahead of her nearest competitor. For if she gets to the mark by sunset, those aboard

Great Bear *is 28 feet 10 inches overall by 26 feet on her waterline by 8 feet 7 inches beam and 1 foot 8 inches draft with the board housed. The mainmast is stepped in a tabernacle for relatively easy lowering.*

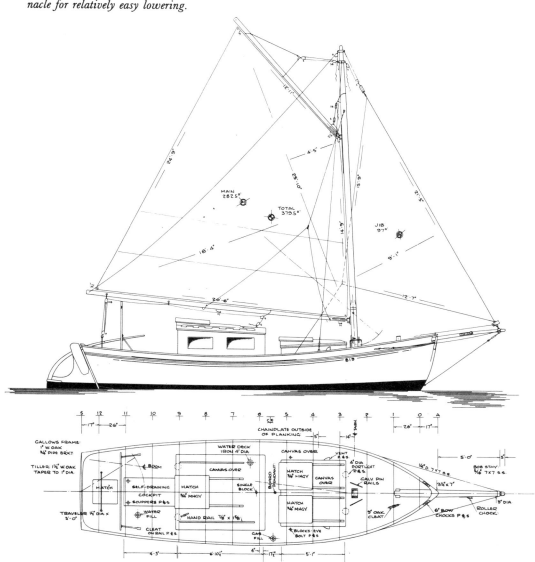

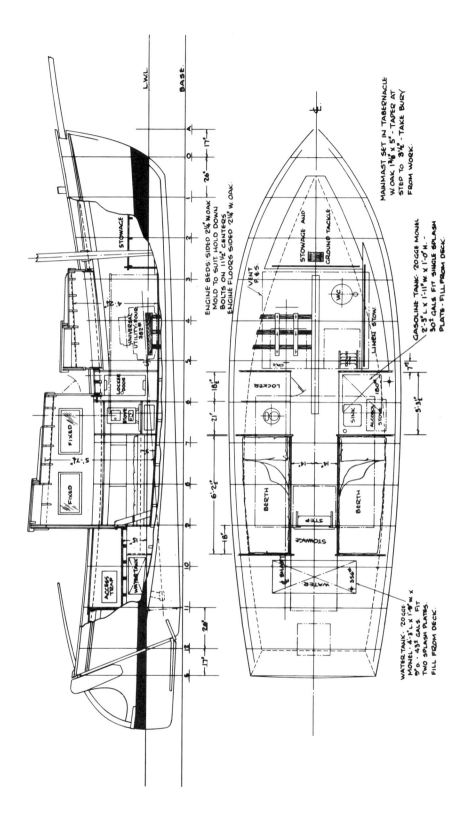

Inboard profile and arrangement of Great Bear. She is arranged for the comfort of two with 5-foot 7 1/4-inch headroom in the after trunk and 4-foot 2 1/4-inch headroom in the forward trunk. The WC is under the forward trunk to starboard, the auxiliary engine to port separated by the centerboard trunk. Obviously, the engine is easily accessible.

Great Bear *on her maiden voyage from Tuckahoe, New Jersey, to her homeport at Forked River. She reflects the desires of Bill Dunn and is a "fun" boat in all respects. (John Atkin photo)*

have enjoyed a happy day afloat, quite content in the company of the gulls and sparkling water. Her design is conceived for poking into creeks and shoals. Her mast is stepped in a tabernacle to be quickly and easily lowered in the event a pleasant waterway lies on the far side of a low highway bridge.

"The 1-foot 8-inch draft, with the board housed, allows her access to many areas that cannot be explored by her long-legged sisters. The flat bottom provides the ability to come to rest in a normal position when the tide, perchance, slides out beneath the bottom . . . ."

Great Bear is now owned by Dayton Trubee, a yacht broker in Bay Head, New Jersey. Like Bill Dunn, Dayton marches to a different drummer and has great affection for the sloop. He has told me she is "the nicest boat [he has] ever owned."

12

—— James Samuel ——

20-foot flat-bottomed catboat

James Samuel was designed originally for Jack Clapp of Greenwich, Connecticut, a good many years ago, and many sisterships have been built by both professional and amateur builders. Several years ago, a long-time friend and client, the late James Maze of Spring Valley, Illinois, wrote to see what we had in the way of a design of a simple boat that would be capable of taking care of herself and in which his grandchildren could learn to sail on the clear waters of Lake Superior.

John Little, of the Mile Creek Boat Shop, Old Lyme, Connecticut (now of Washington, Maine), built *James Samuel* for Maze. John did his usual creditable work and the Maze family was delighted with the boat. She is still used by Pete Loveland, Maze's son-in-law. *James Samuel* is kept at the Mazes' summer home at Eagle Harbor, Wisconsin, along with a Sea Bright skiff we designed for them about 25 years ago! The skiff, named the *Sallie Hyde,* at last word still had her original four-cylinder Gray engine.

James Samuel is 20 feet 1 inch overall by 19 feet on her waterline by 7 feet 2 inches beam and 7 inches draft with the centerboard housed. The freeboard is 2 feet 7 inches at the bow and 2 feet at the stern. It is obvious that she is truly a big skiff, a load-carrier of considerable ability and an all-around practical boat.

Many skiffs are too wide on their bottoms, or they have too much (or too little) rocker and inadequate flare on their topsides. A vertical-sided skiff is dangerous, notwithstanding the philosophy of my "naval artichoke" friend Phil Bolger out of Gloucester, Massachusetts. They lack reserve stability and the ability to throw water away from the gunwales when underway. A skiff with excessive flare in her topsides is difficult to build. Perhaps this is the reason so many of the slab-sided type are built. The sections of *James Samuel* incorporate sufficient flare to provide reserve stability but not so much that building is difficult.

James Samuel has a big rudder. All flat-bottomed centerboarders require a big rudder and a suitable skeg — the former brings her about quickly and the latter helps her jog along on a straight course.

Our big skiff is cat-rigged, with a simple and practical sail plan. The mast is raked rather sharply — 15 inches in 10 feet. In the interest of economy, it may be gotten out of a grown stick of spruce or fir. Since this kind of mast has an unfortunate tendency to "walk" out of shape unless very well seasoned, it is practical to rip a rectangular-section stick in half. Turn the halves around, end-for-end, and glue these up with Resorcinol or another *time-proven* glue. (Incidentally, I have received some negative reports on various epoxies — and I have observed some failures first-hand.)

The mast's diameter is 4½ inches at the sheer and 2½ inches at the top, with a fair, even taper from sheer to top. The length from sheer to top is 24 feet. Add to this the bury — the distance from the sheer to the bottom of the step — and the total is 26 feet 4 inches. There is only a single headstay and no shrouds are required.

The boom is 16 feet 7 inches long, 3 inches in diameter, and tapers to 2½ inches at its forward and after ends. The specified wooden jaws and mast hoops are the utmost in simplicity — and minimal cost.

The sail area is 164 square feet. While this is modest, it is comfortable for easy handling. There are two rows of reef points and no battens. For beginners in sail and for folks who sail purely for fun, *James Samuel* has a lot to offer.

She has plenty of room for five or six people — or more, as shown in the photograph — and is an ideal boat for a children's training program in camping and overnight cruising and for use as a yacht club tender and a safe rental skiff. There are two thwarts, stern sheets, and side seats.

James Samuel's ample breadth provides good stability, which allows her to carry the sail well. With her high freeboard, she is dry and safe. In a boat of this breadth, the centerboard trunk is not particularly in the way.

Sail plan and interior arrangement of
James Samuel. *Her rig is the utmost
in practical simplicity.*

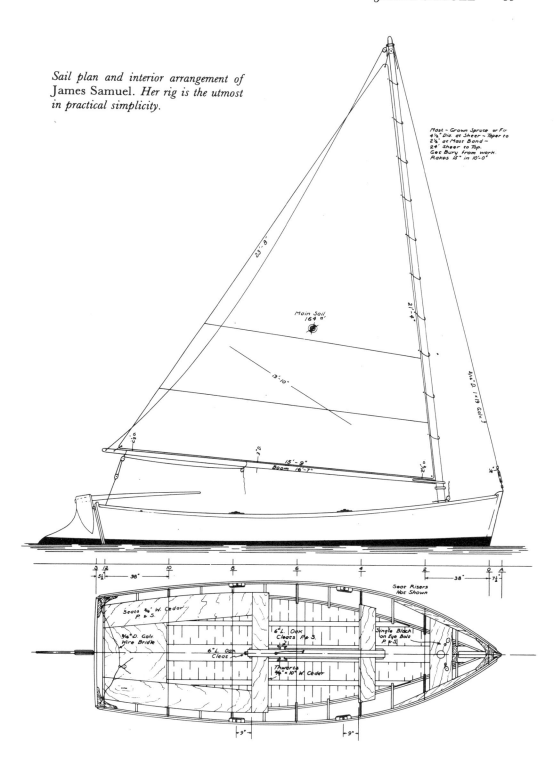

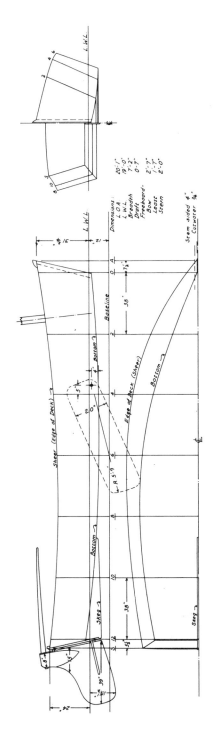

Lines drawings of the 20-foot flat-bottomed sailing skiff James Samuel.

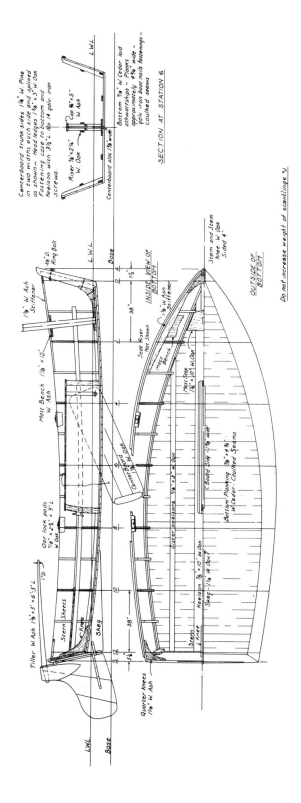

Construction drawing — inboard profile, construction plan of interior, outside of bottom and section. Complete working drawings include a section indicating plywood.

Eight members of the Maze family sail on Lake Superior aboard James Samuel *off Eagle Harbor, Wisconsin.*

And since the board is long, it does not need to be lowered much more than is indicated on the drawings. Some experimenting with its vertical position will indicate the proper depth for balancing the boat under sail as well as preventing sliding to leeward.

Equipment should include: nicely fashioned spruce oars, an approved lifejacket (flotation device) for each person aboard, a long-lasting flashlight, an 8-pound Danforth anchor, 150 feet of ⅜-inch-diameter Dacron rode, a wood scoop or bailer to be made fast to the boat with a lanyard, and a single 3-pound dry chemical fire extinguisher if an outboard motor is used for auxiliary power. The motor need not be greater than 4 or 5 horsepower and should be installed on a fixed bracket to port of the rudder.

It is always useful to have a spare length of line aboard, and I would advise carrying 150 to 200 feet of ½-inch-diameter synthetic line for towing or other emergencies. She does not require running lights when under sail; simply beam the flashlight on her sail if another boat is approaching or nearby. A combination running light is required if the boat is operated with the outboard engine. It is a good idea to have one, even though it is not required while under sail.

If the boat is to be out of the water a good deal of the time, which is probably unlikely in view of her size, it might prove practical to use waterproof marine plywood for her bottom. Rotary-cut Bruynzeel mahogany is excellent, although expensive. It has a solid core and is fine material in all respects. Any grade of 100 percent marine plywood, with its solid core, will be entirely satisfactory. Over the years, I've seen a great deal of plywood. My father and L. Francis Herreshoff, as well as other experienced designers, took a "dim view of the stuff." My father felt that its only purpose was for the bottom of drawers. L. Francis didn't think it was good for anything. I do not disagree with their wisdom, nor do I feel that plywood is any better than it was 50 years ago. With all due respect, however, it does have its practical applications in this day and age. It is difficult to find first-class traditional boatbuilding woods, and marine plywood is an acceptable substitute. Do be certain, however, that it is 100 percent marine plywood; do not accept "exterior grade." This will prove to be disappointing in a relatively short period of time — and far too much time and money are already involved with building a boat.

The plywood construction section of *James Samuel* included in the working drawings indicates the scantlings and materials. There is also a large-scale drawing of the stem and its rabbet.

13

— Schatze —

7-foot 10-inch pram

I was pleased when my friend W.H. (''Ham'') deFontaine asked me to undertake the design of a little pram for his own use — to be published by *Yachting* magazine. The design and the wonderfully clear ''how-to-build'' photographs appeared in the June 1968 issue.

My father designed Ham's original pram, *Rinky Dink,* in 1924. It was not easy to improve on this grand boat. *Rinky Dink* is 7 feet overall. I increased the length of the new pram 10 inches and her beam just slightly; I added more freeboard and increased the sheer. Thus my design is more burdensome.

Ham had named the new pram *Feather* when the design appeared in *Yachting.* I did not feel that the name did justice to the boat, so I changed it to *Schatze* — a ''little treasure.'' Her principal dimensions are 7 feet 10 inches overall by 3 feet 7½ inches beam and 3 inches draft. *Schatze* is built of ¼-inch marine plywood rather than by the traditional method of planking specified for *Rinky Dink.*

The article in *Yachting* stirred up a great deal of interest, and I have sold well over 100 sets of her working drawings. These include an isometric drawing of her building form, or jig, in addition to complete details and dimensions.

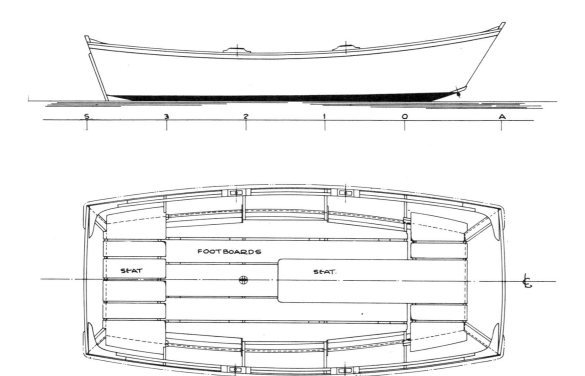

Profile and arrangement of Schatze — *a little treasure* — *7 feet 10 inches overall by 3 feet 7½ inches in breadth and 3 inches draft. A flat-bottomed pram constructed of two 4-foot by 8-foot sheets of waterproof marine plywood. The pram was designed for W.H. (''Ham'') deFontaine, associate editor of* Yachting *magazine, and was published in that magazine. Interest in building the pram continues, and many of the boats have been built over the years.*

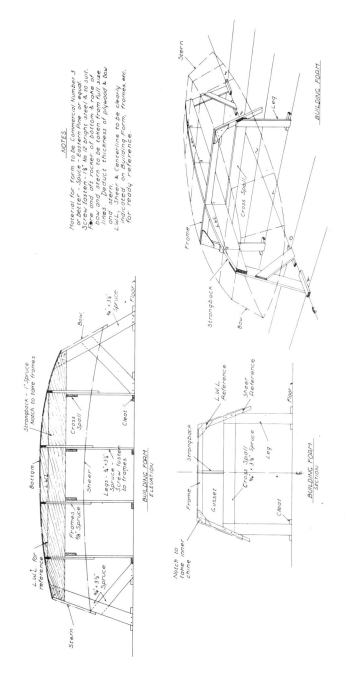

NOTES

Material for form to be Commercial Number 3
or better - Spruce - Eastern Pine or equal.
Screw fasten - 1¼" No.12 bright steel & to suit.
Fore and aft rocker of bottom & rake of
bow and stern to be taken from full size
lines. Deduct thickness of plywood & bow
and stern.
L.W.L., Sheer & Centerline to be clearly
indicated on Building Form, Frames, etc.
for ready reference.

Stern

Stern

Frame

Strongback

Cross Spall

Bow

Bow

Leg

BUILDING FORM

Bow

**Strongback - 1" Spruce
Notch to take frames**

Bottom

L.W.L.

Cross Spall

Sheer

**Legs - ¾ × 3½
Spruce -
Screw fasten
to frames**

**¾" × 3½"
Spruce**

Floor

**BUILDING FORM
ELEVATION**

**L.W.L. for
reference**

**Frames
¾" Spruce**

**¾" × 3½"
Spruce**

Cleat

Stern

**Notch to
take inner
chine**

Frame

Gusset

Strongback

**L.W.L.
Reference**

**Sheer
Reference**

**Cross Spall
¾" × 3½" Spruce**

Leg

Floor

Cleat

**BUILDING FORM
SECTION**

Elevation, section, and isometric drawing of the building form of Schatze.

The original 7-foot Rinky Dink, *designed in 1924! She was built by Richard Smith at Liverpool, England, in 1981.*

Schatze, *built by Iver Lofving of Katonah, New York. Lofving, an architect, had never built a boat before, and he had such a grand time that he began work on the more complicated* Cabin Boy. *It is evident that he has done a fine piece of work.*

A letter typical of many I've received is from LCDR Nancy Crosby, Navy nurse, whose father built one of the prams for her. She has written, "Enclosed is a picture of *Schatze* my Dad built this winter. She is remarkably light in the water and carries a good distance when you stop rowing. She tows beautifully astern of our 22-foot Sailmaster sailboat. Many thanks for the plans. Dad considered it quite a challenge and enjoyed building the boat."

In the construction of *Schatze,* the chine members must be sawn to the shape in elevation. If the builder tries to bend them to the curve shown, they will twist and develop a "knuckle."

SCHATZE
By W.H. deFontaine, 1968

It all started a good many years ago before the days of waterproof plywood and the advent of the V-bottomed pram. I had a little 7-foot flat-bottomed pram, designed by Billy Atkin and built very lightly with Philippine mahogany planking about ⅜ inch thick. She towed well, rowed well, and carried three people and some gear — altogether a most useful and satisfactory tender. Remembering this handy and easy-to-build little boat, I asked Billy's son, John, to design me another as nearly like the original as he could — primarily, I think, in order to prove that a flat-bottomed pram was as good, if not better, than a V-bottomed one, and a lot easier to build.

Of course we took advantage of all the wonderful new materials that have been developed in the last 25 years, so the new boat is planked with U.S. Plywood's ¼-inch mahogany plywood over spruce frames, and most joints are glued with Elmer's waterproof glue and fastened with Anchorfast Monel nails.

Because a joint made with Elmer's glue is virtually unbreakable, and there is always the outside chance that some day a boat may need a new bottom or topside planks, we decided to set these in neoprene bedding compound with great adhesive properties as well as a certain amount of elasticity. In addition, these panels were Anchorfast-nailed. And that was not all. Since this boat was more or less of a test job, we decided — my son-in-law Irv Westermann and I — to give her the works. So we covered her chines and the bottom joints fore and aft with 3-inch fiberglass tape set in polyester resin. Then, to arm the bottom against abrasion on beach stones or floats and to protect it permanently against marine borers, we covered it with Dynel cloth set in the same resin. This cloth is carried up the side only far enough to cover the fiberglass tape. The result is a light boat and a very strong one. And, of course, she is absolutely tight.

Wade ("Ham") deFontaine was an associate editor of Yachting *magazine for nearly 20 years. Being an ardent yachtsman — and individualist — and a self-taught yacht designer, he brought to* Yachting *a great many talents that, over the years, left their unmistakable mark.*

Even though we knew borers couldn't get at the bottom, we didn't want to establish a barnacle boarding house, so we painted her bottom with Salem Paint Company's antifouling red, which Sandy Moffat recommended so highly — and it turned out just as represented. To finish her off like the handsome little boat she is, we gave her four coats of varnish — adding some fine pumice powder to the final coat on her floorboards to make them nonskid.

For a painter I rigged a length of ½-inch-diameter, three-strand nylon rope through a ½-inch hole bored in the bow transom well above the waterline. Inside the transom is a heavy leather washer on the line, which terminates in a wall and crown. To keep out the water, I filled the interstices between rope and hole with neoprene. Simple, neat, economical, and effective. I used a piece of 1-inch-diameter nylon rope to stretch around her gunwales for a fender — a handsome finishing touch.

Of course she has a pair of brass rowlocks, but with four sockets — two forward, two aft. This allows the oarsman to move his weight to the best position on the fore-and-aft seat to balance the boat properly, depending on the load.

When launching day came, we put her on top of the car and took her down to the water. Because Irv was really her builder, it seemed appropriate to let him have the first row. We tried her with two aboard —

Irv and his son Bill, a husky young fellow who had helped in her building. Finally all three of us climbed in. She was buoyant as a cork, rowed easily, with good fetches between strokes, and spun on a dime. In a word, she handled beautifully, fully meeting our expectations. Just to convince ourselves that she would tow well, we went for an hour's sail in the *Saucy Kate,* my jaunty Bahama dinghy, and towed the pram. She followed us like a duck, with absolutely no appreciable drag on her painter — the final reward for a job well done.

14

—— Ninigret ——

22-foot V-bottomed bassboat

I designed the 22-foot *Ninigret* skiff for Dudley Slocum of Casey Key, Nakomis, Florida. "Dud" wanted a practical fishing boat to use both in Florida and at his summer home at Arnolda, Rhode Island, which borders on Ninigret Pond — which, in turn, extends through a narrow inlet into the waters of Block Island Sound. It is here that Dudley wanted to troll, parallel to the shoreline, for the elusive striped bass and bluefish. Above all, we were interested in developing an easily driven hull that would behave herself in Block Island Sound and in the Gulf off his Casey Key home.

Since this design has never before been published, I am interested in knowing what sort of reception it will receive.

Ninigret's principal dimensions are 22 feet ¼ inch overall by 20 feet on her waterline by 6 feet 8 inches beam and 1 foot draft. She is constructed of ⅜-inch rotary-cut Bruynzeel waterproof plywood over ⅝-inch by 2½-inch white oak frames spaced on the stations. Power is an Evinrude 30 h.p. outboard engine and the efficiently driven hull goes just over 18 m.p.h. with this unit. Dudley used greater horsepower on his boat simply to experiment and see which power plant suited her — and what she could handle. He has used a 45 h.p. engine successfully.

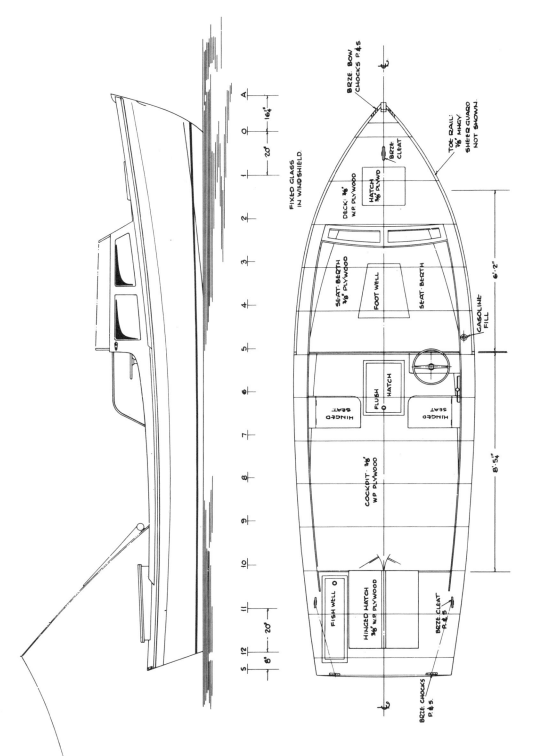

Profile and arrangement of Dudley Slocum's 22-foot Ninigret, a bassboat. The forward cockpit makes a fine fishing platform. Two berths and a WC on the centerline provide accommodations for overnight cruising.

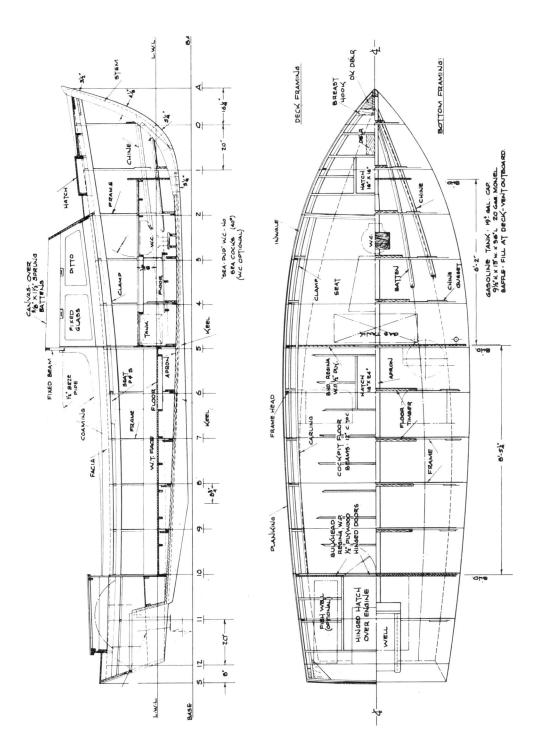

Construction drawings of the Ninigret. Frames are spaced on the stations. The outboard motor is located in a well with hinged hatches and doors.

A quartering view of the Ninigret *showing the opening in the transom and the hinged box over the motor.*

The canvas cuddy top is supported by sprung ash battens. The WC is on the centerline tucked under the V-berths. Engine controls are to starboard with the wheel on the vertical bulkhead.

I am not enamored of a huge outboard engine hung on the stern of an offshore fishing boat, so the 30 h.p. engine is installed in a well — and an enclosed compartment. This was an amazingly good solution. It is possible to carry on a normal conversation when the boat is underway — and she slides through the water with a minimum of fuss.

Ninigret's arrangement shows two camping berths with a WC tucked between them on the hull centerline. There is a removable canvas "top" on the cuddy overhead, and when it is removed, the seats make a fine fishing platform for Dudley's trolling. The steering station is shown to starboard with the wheel standing parallel to the cuddy bulkhead. This is far more practical than the more usual centerline console with little or nothing to lean against in a seaway.

A man named John Martindale of Olmstead, Ohio, built one of the *Ninigret* skiffs several years ago and wrote me an encouraging letter. "I can't tell you how pleased I am with the *Ninigret* skiff. Its performance is excellent, and the very many compliments I have received from people who know boats are due to her designer as well as her builder . . . . The steering system is Morse and handles very well. She planes very easily in quiet water, and in rough Lake Erie waves, the sharp forefoot creates a soft, dry ride." It is this type of letter that tends to make everything worthwhile.

Dudley Slocum has now owned the *Ninigret* for 20 years, and from time to time, he calls me to tell me what a fine boat she is. I must reciprocate by saying that he has been a fine friend over these many years.

15

—— Finkeldink ——

9-foot pram

One of the most rewarding aspects of designing wholesome boats is the character of the client who comes through the door of Anchordown. William Colihan of Essex, Connecticut, is one of our very special clients! And the story of his *Finkeldink* requires an introduction.

Several years ago I designed a practical, wholesome, deadrise 36-foot powerboat for Bill. He outlined his requirements in simple terms: a straightforward V-bottomed displacement hull to replace one I had designed several years earlier for Tom Robins of Darien, Connecticut.

Robins' 36-footer was a twin-screw displacement powerboat with two big, heavy Gray gasoline engines. She was built by Jim Richardson at Cambridge, Maryland. The two Grays specified by Robins provided far more power than the hull could use. Thus, through no direct fault of mine — other than following the dictates of my client — she was not entirely successful. Unfortunately, she was destroyed in a fire at Essex. Bill Colihan, who owned the boat at that time, wanted her duplicated. Being a more flexible and tolerant man than Tom Robins, he took my advice and we installed a single 80 h.p. Lehman/Ford diesel. The new boat — which he named *Ulsworthy* — provides him with economy of operation and, I am pleased to say, has come up to everyone's expectations.

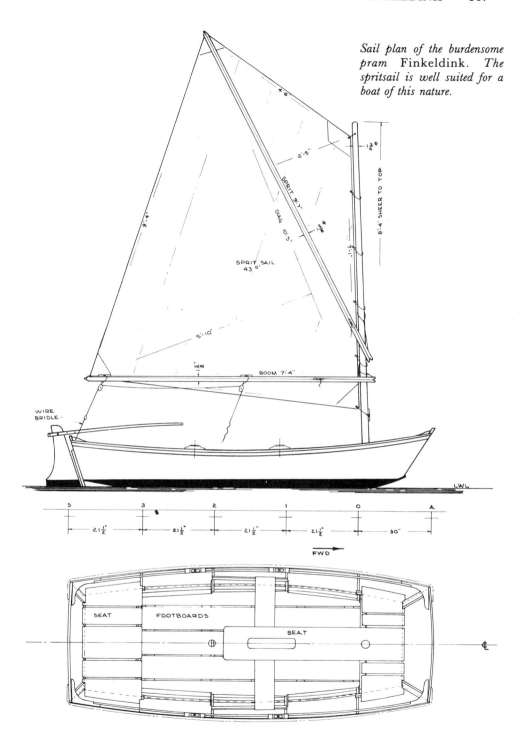

Sail plan of the burdensome pram Finkeldink. *The spritsail is well suited for a boat of this nature.*

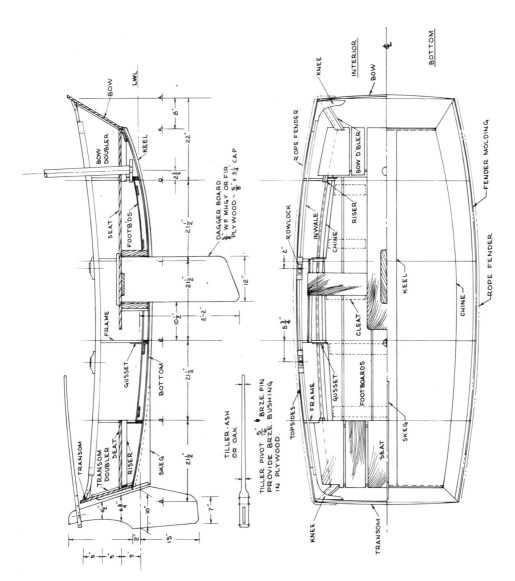

BOW

LWL

BOW DOUBLER

KEEL

SEAT

FOOTB'DS

DAGGER BOARD
⅝" WP MHGY OR FIR
PLYWOOD ~ ⅝" x 3¼" CAP

FRAME

GUSSET

BOTTOM

TRANSOM

TRANSOM DOUBLER

SEAT

RISER

SKEG

8"

22"

2¾"

2½"

2½"

10½"

2½"

3

2½"

4½"

6¾"

10"

7"

2"

15"

5"   5"   5"

12"

2-2"

TILLER-ASH OR OAK

TILLER PIVOT 5⁄16" BRZE. PIN
PROVIDE BRZE. BUSHING
IN PLYWOOD

KNEE

INTERIOR

BOW

BOTTOM

ROPE FENDER

BOW D'BLER

INWALE

ROWLOCK

RISER

CHINE

CLEAT

FENDER MOLDING

KEEL

ROPE FENDER

CHINE

FRAME

GUSSET

FOOTBOARDS

TOPSIDES

SKEG

SEAT

TRANSOM

KNEE

2"

5¾"

Construction elevation and plan of the 9-foot Finkeldink. Her large daggerboard and rudder come in handy in going to windward.

Finkeldink is a 9-foot overall pram designed for Bill Colihan and built by Art Finkeldey of Essex, Connecticut. The pram is an enlarged version of Schatze.

Two or three years ago, Bill was heading into Thunderbolt Marina, in Georgia, aboard the boat. There were two men watching him come into his slip. When he was tied up and comfortable, the men came over to see *Ulsworthy.* "Is she an Atkin design?" one of the men asked. Bill acknowledged that she was. "I thought so," said the man, who turned to his friend and said, "You owe me 10 dollars." These are the kinds of boats I like to design — nothing commonplace about them. Unusual, yes, but not commonplace.

In 1981 Bill Winterer, owner of the Griswold Inn at Essex, invited several of us — including Bill Colihan and Britton Chance — for luncheon. We carried on a lively conversation about boats — and boat designs. Britton has designed some unusual IOR-influenced racing machines, and I told him that I felt some of them were rather homely. I can't say that he agreed with me, and I acknowledge that my designs may be "unusual," but I don't think any of them are as homely as some of Britton's creations!

Bill Colihan asked me to design a pram for the davits on the stern of *Ulsworthy.* She had to be burdensome, for the Colihans are large people: Bill's son, Alston, is 6 feet 8 inches tall. I used the design of *Schatze* and pulled her up to 9 feet overall by 7 feet 1⅜ inches on her waterline by 3 feet 10½ inches beam and 3 inches draft. She is built of ¼-inch waterproof plywood and has 43 square feet of sail area in the sprit rig.

The boat was built by the late A.J. Finkeldey, of Essex — the last boat this talented builder put together — and Bill Colihan named her *Finkeldink.* She is a fine piece of work — and a design that meets the needs of the Colihans very nicely.

16

—— Bruce Conklin* ——

15-foot 6-inch rowing (pulling) boat

In recent years there has been growing interest in pulling boats — Whitehalls and other graceful rowing craft that slide through the water with a minimum of effort and little fuss. Truly delightful hulls possessing grace and charm.

In 1943 my father designed the pulling boat *Bruce Conklin*. The boat was named after an old shipmate, a friend of all the Atkin family. Bruce taught me to sail at Huntington, New York, when I was eight years old. We spent a great deal of time together around the water. First we sailed in the Suicide (Development) Class boats at Huntington and later we were both employed by the Luders Marine Construction Company, at Stamford, Connecticut. In our free time we would spend hours trolling for striped bass off the end of Long Neck Point. Bruce was an excellent architect but fundamentally, like many old-fashioned Long Islanders, he was a waterman, familiar with the ways of Nature. Hunting and fishing gave purpose to his being. I learned a great deal from Bruce Conklin.

When my father designed the pulling boat *Bruce Conklin* he wrote, "This boat was designed with a view to producing a useful craft at summer camps, fishing places, mountain lakes, rivers, and the great salt seas

---

The design of Bruce Conklin *is published with the permission of Hearst Marine Books, New York.*

— any place where an easily rowed and burdensome small boat is needed for business or pleasure purposes. *Bruce Conklin* was designed especially for rowing, but I will have no quarrel with those who wish to propel the boat with an outboard motor of modest horsepower. However, do not use a big motor; three horsepower is ample for speeds up to seven miles an hour. Above this the stern will settle badly, because it is sharp and the after buttock lines rise abruptly. The form is perfect for rowing and for speeds under seven miles an hour.

"It will be especially noticed that the keel is straight for its entire length. Also that it projects below the garboard planks 1 inch. The purpose of the long, straight keel is to keep the boat on a true course while under way with oars, and to prevent it from walking all over the place when at anchor. This is exactly the opposite performance one looks for in a small tender or dinghy, which only goes to show that one type of boat cannot serve every purpose. A boat like *Bruce Conklin* will be difficult to tow because it will yaw badly and end up by capsizing if towed fast in rough water. And by the same token it will be unhandy as a dinghy because it will not turn sharply and quickly.

"*Bruce Conklin* is a boat that will be easily pulled by oars and easily kept on its course in smooth or rough water, with, across, or against the wind and sea. The body plan shows firm, strong bilges along the middle sections, which means the boat will not flop this way and that when weights are shifted off the centerline. The bow and stern will take to the sea kindly. Coupled with the fact that the boat will be easily rowed by one man, she should be ideal for trolling for fish. This, in fact, is the first purpose I had in mind for the boat. Rowing is dreadfully hard work in practically all the boats designed for propulsion with an outboard motor.

"Bruce Conklin, my best shipmate and one of years standing, is an amateur fisherman. He has that elusive sense that tells where the bass, weakfish, and bluefish are likely to be found; and he usually finds them. All summer long after working hours, my shipmate, with my son John and some other indispensable technical men, have been fishing the waters of Long Neck, the rocks off Pratt Island, and the place where the water rushes into the old Cove Mill Pond. It is a long row out to the haunts of the fish, so it was usually late before the boys returned. As a measure of appreciation of a good and true shipmate, then, you know why I have named this design *Bruce Conklin*."

The boat is 15 feet 6 inches overall by 15 feet on the waterline by 3 feet 9 inches beam. She has a draft of 6 inches. Freeboard at her bow is 1 foot 8¼ inches and at the stern 1 foot 3¼ inches. The arrangement shows three thwarts without the usual stern sheets. For trolling fish with two, the man with the fishing rod sits aft, the oarsman sits forward. With two

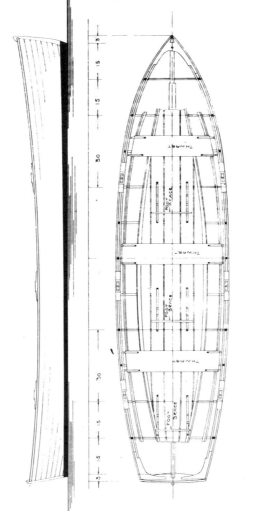

The outboard profile and deck plan for the pulling boat Bruce Conklin. She is 15 feet 6 inches overall by 3 feet 9 inches beam and has a draft of 6 inches. She has the ability to slide through the water without fuss.

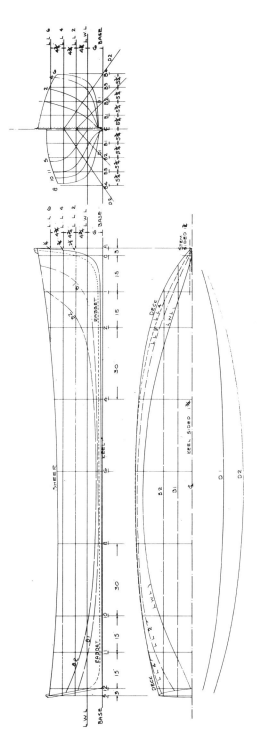

Lines of the graceful pulling boat Bruce Conklin.

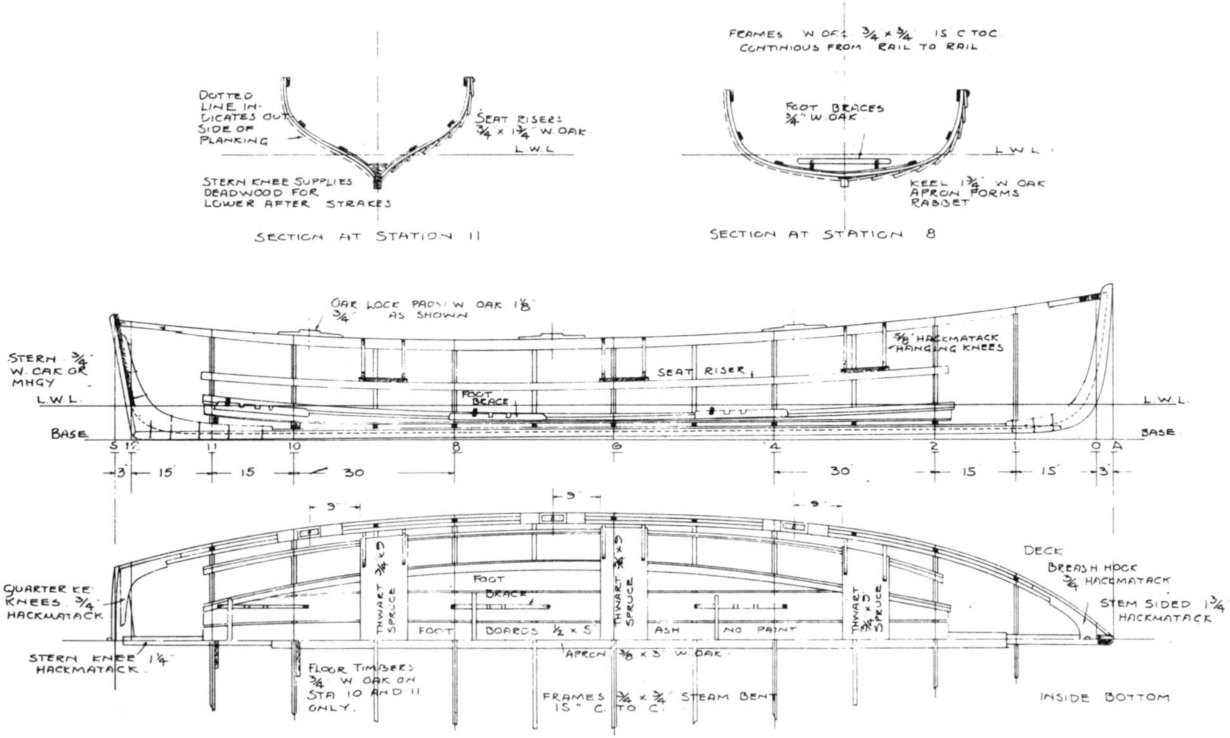
DOTTED LINE INDICATES OUTSIDE OF PLANKING
SEAT RISERS 3/4 x 1 3/4" W. OAK
L.W.L
STERN KNEE SUPPLIES DEADWOOD FOR LOWER AFTER STRAKES
SECTION AT STATION 11
FRAMES W. OAK 3/4 x 3/4 15 C TO C CONTINUOUS FROM RAIL TO RAIL
FOOT BRACES 3/4" W. OAK
KEEL 1 3/4 W. OAK
APRON FORMS RABBET
SECTION AT STATION 8
OAR LOCK PADS W. OAK 1 1/8 3/4 AS SHOWN
5/8 HACKMATACK HANGING KNEES
STERN 3/4 W. OAK OR MHGY
SEAT RISER
FOOT BRACE
L.W.L.
BASE
DECK
BREASH HOOK 3/4 HACKMATACK
STEM SIDED 1 3/4 HACKMATACK
QUARTER KNEES 3/4 HACKMATACK
THWART 3/4 x 9 SPRUCE
FOOT BRACE
FOOT BOARDS 1/2 x 5
ASH
NO PAINT
STERN KNEE 1 1/4 HACKMATACK
APRON 3/8 x 3 W. OAK
FLOOR TIMBERS 3/4 W. OAK ON STA 10 AND 11 ONLY.
FRAMES 3/4 x 3/4 STEAM BENT 15" C. TO C.
INSIDE BOTTOM

Construction drawings for the Bruce Conklin, *with sections at stations 8 and 11.*

The 15-foot 6-inch Bruce Conklin, *built by the gentleman with his oars at rest. He obviously did a fine piece of work in building this delightful boat.*

fishing, the third man sits amidships. Alone, one rows from the center thwart. So the hull is always in good balance. Suitable foot braces are screwed to the footboards and have adjustable cross members as shown. There should be no paint or varnish on the footboards. Left bare, the wood will not be slippery. It is hard work rowing without proper braces for the feet. The thwarts are well below the gunwales to make it easier to row, and the oak rowlock sockets are just 9 inches abaft the after edges of the thwarts. These features make a big difference in the way a rowing boat handles.

17

— Cabin Boy —

7-foot 6-inch flat-bottomed skiff

An entire book has been written on the skiff *Cabin Boy. Building the Skiff Cabin Boy* by Clemens C. Kuhlig, published by International Marine Publishing Company, is a comprehensive, well-written coverage of the little boat — so there is not a great deal that I can add. But I can bring you up to date on this little hooker.

The principal dimensions of *Cabin Boy* are 7 feet 6 inches overall by 3 feet 10 inches beam and 3¾ inches draft. The interest in *Cabin Boy* has been overwhelming since the book was published, for she is just the right size tender for the average auxiliary — and, from all indications, she presents a boatbuilding challenge that many folks feel they can meet. I have received orders for some 150 sets of plans for *Cabin Boy* from all over the world.

My friend Captain John S. Hart of Marblehead, Massachusetts, who is retired from American Airlines, builds little boats as an avocation. He built *Cabin Boy* and wrote, in connection with the boat, "I received a call today from Tom Duburing, the wooden boatbuilding instructor at the Boston Museum of Transportation.

"The subject of *Cabin Boy* came up and he restated that she was the

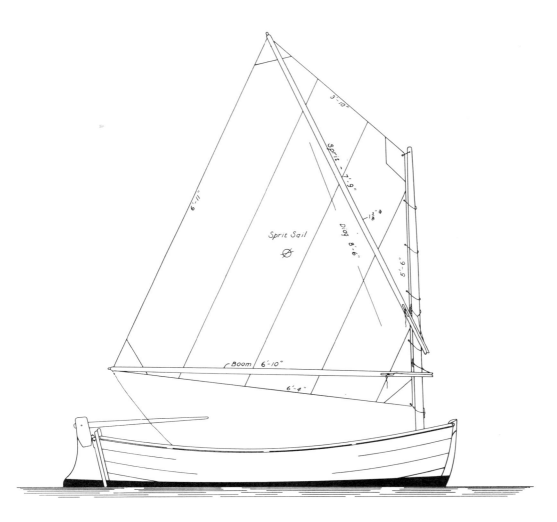

A sprit rig, the ultimate in simplicity, combined with a daggerboard and rudder, transforms Cabin Boy *to a sailing boat. Despite her modest dimensions, the hull is burdensome, and a skipper can enjoy the waning hours of a summer's day in his favorite harbor. All drawings of* Cabin Boy *were traced by Ted Smith, whose assistance I appreciate.*

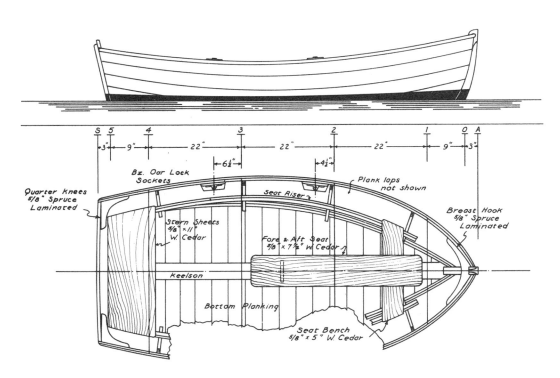

Profile and arrangement of Cabin Boy. *As in* Schatze *and* Petey Dink, *the seat extends fore-and-aft, which is a very practical arrangement that allows the shifting of weight of the oarsman and crew.*

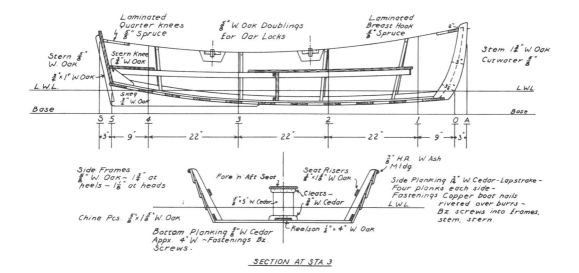

Construction drawings of the Cabin Boy. She is 7 feet 6 inches overall by 3 feet 10 inches in breadth and draws 3¾ inches. Cabin Boy will weigh about 70 pounds if built of good-quality white cedar as specified.

The hull form of Cabin Boy ready for the application of Airex foam, which will be covered inside and out with a single layer of 10-ounce chrome glass cloth impregnated with epoxy resin. Her builder is using the Airex method to gain experience with the material and has reported very successful results.

Bill Tillman of Coral Gables, Florida, built his Sand Dollar *to the design of* Cabin Boy. *He used waterproof plywood ¼ inch thick for her topsides and underbody. The little boat is virtually complete — she requires only the fitting and fastening of her sheer guard and suitable flotation.* Sand Dollar *is a first-class example of the high-quality work produced by competent amateur builders.*

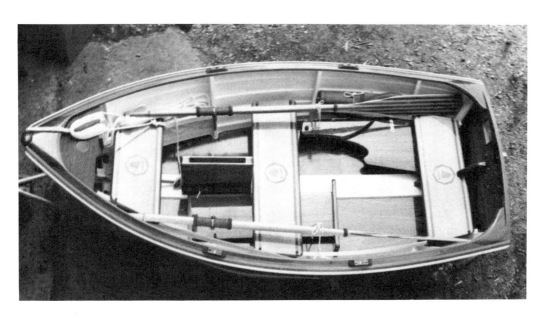

The ultimate in perfection! Clem Kuhlig's Cabin Boy *viewed from aloft. The designs in her thwarts are inlaid mahogany. The details are beyond description, the workmanship indescribably wonderful. Kuhlig, a relatively young toolmaker, also undertook the building of the 12-foot* Pocahontas *from our designs, and she, too, is perfection.*

most handsome and finest performing boat he had ever rowed. He said you could row *Cabin Boy* with a teaspoon, and, for a little boat, she carries her way between strokes in a surprising fashion.

"I thought his comments were very complimentary and I humbly agree."

Another letter, from Bill Tillman of Coral Gables, Florida, is also encouraging. Tillman wrote, "I finally completed *Cabin Boy* early this month. I used ¼-inch waterproof plywood. Otherwise followed your specifications pretty faithfully . . . and I'm very satisfied with her. She rows well even in a chop and tows beautifully astern of my Columbia 24."

I feel fortunate in having a good many similar letters, and naturally it is rewarding to know that the little *Cabin Boy* has come up to expectations.

She can be built strictly for rowing, as illustrated, or a simple sprit rig and daggerboard can be installed for youngsters learning the ways of small sailing boats.

18

—— Elon Jessup ——

16-foot 6⅜-inch flat-bottomed outboard

A long time ago I was in Woods Hole, Massachusetts, and visited my old friend the late Elon Jessup. Elon used to stop by *Motor Boating*'s booth at the annual New York Boat Show, where I worked for some 20 years, and we would always enjoy a chat about boats and the water. He was a genuine person, and I was pleased to have the opportunity to see him at Woods Hole, where he was sitting in a small cottage knocking out his monthly article for *Hunting and Fishing* magazine. The simplicity of his cottage and his mode of living — the activity that kept things going — greatly impressed me. I felt this was close to the ideal means of earning a living. Elon Jessup made a great impression on me, so I decided to try to follow his example — writing and designing small boats. Aside from my father, Elon Jessup possibly was a greater influence on my future than anyone else I had met.

I designed the 16-foot flat-bottomed fishing skiff shown here for Thomas Massey of Houston, Texas. The simplicity of the skiff seems in keeping with Elon Jessup — so I named the design for him.

The principal dimensions of *Elon Jessup* are 16 feet 6⅜ inches overall by 15 feet on her waterline by 5 feet 4½ inches beam and 6½ inches draft. A

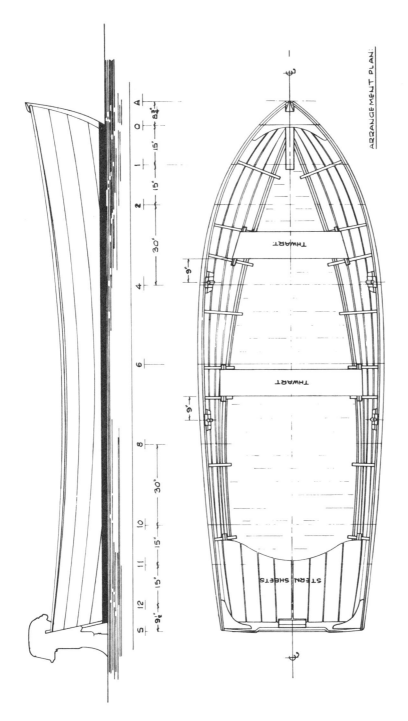

ARRANGEMENT PLAN.

Outboard profile and arrangement of Elon Jessup. Her engine should be no bigger than 10 to 12 horsepower.

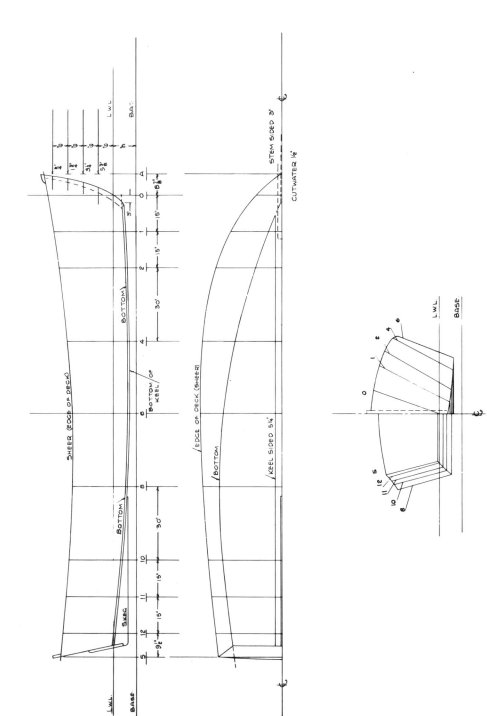

Lines drawings of the Elon Jessup. She is relatively narrow but has considerable flare full length. The flare forward will keep her dry in any kind of chop.

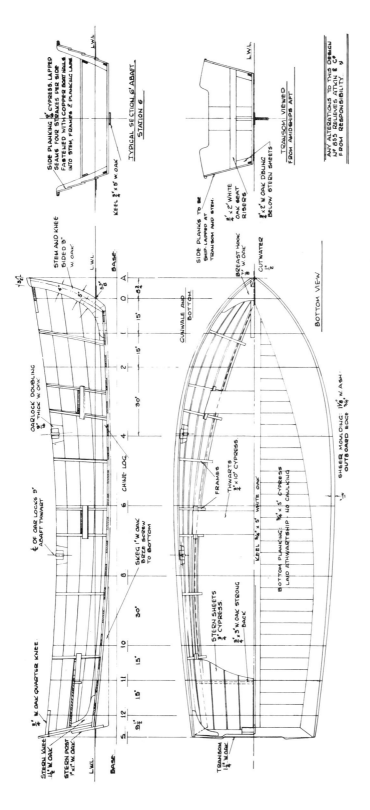

Construction drawings of the 16-foot 6⅜-inch Elon Jessup. Like many of the flat-
bottomed boats in this portfolio of designs, this one can be built of waterproof plywood — in
this instance, ½-inch rotary-cut Bruynzeel.

Elon Jessup. His daughter has written: "He was not a great and famous man, he was a good and kind man who made his living writing about his friends and their boats."

The flat-bottomed, outboard-powered skiff Elon Jessup *in the garden of her builder's lovely boatshop. A simple, straightforward boat for fishing and simply messing about on the water.*

Tom Massey's grand boatbuilding shop in Houston, Texas.

10 or 12 h.p. outboard motor will provide ample power for her to slide along at 16 or 17 miles per hour. The engine is hung on the transom. A long tiller can be arranged to steer the boat from the center thwart, which makes a simple, practical arrangement.

The lines indicate a relatively narrow hull with sufficient rocker to accommodate the outboard, but she won't handle any more than that. She has nice flare, and other than slapping going to windward in a chop, the hull will be comfortable and dry.

Elon Jessup is shown outside Massey's handsome Royal Barry Wills boatshop. A strong painter is led through holes just abaft her stem — once again, a simple and practical arrangement. It is evident that Massey has done a fine piece of work in putting together the 16-footer.

19

—— Tom Davin ——

20-foot ¾-inch flat-bottomed skiff

The late Tom Davin was one of the most inspiring men and *the* most inspiring editor I have ever known. Tom was a joy to be with, and we spent lots of time together. I am fortunate to have known him.

Many years ago, before the present-day term "gridlock" was conceived, my wife, Pat, Tom Davin, and I were returning from a trip to Maryland. Approaching the George Washington Bridge, we were stopped in traffic and remained so for hours. As we crept slowly to the bridge, Tom observed, "The end of the world will come when Detroit builds one too many cars and all the toilets in the country stop functioning at the same time!" Tom is immortalized in our memories by his keen foresight — which is one reason that I carry a galvanized bucket in the trunk of my car.

The 20-foot *Tom Davin* closely approaches the kind of boat I am going to have built for myself some day by my friend Bob Wilmes at East Haddam, Connecticut.

She was designed for Tom Massey of Houston, Texas, and her principal dimensions are 20 feet ¾ inch overall by 18 feet 9 inches on the waterline by 6 feet 2 inches beam and 1 foot 7 inches draft. A Universal

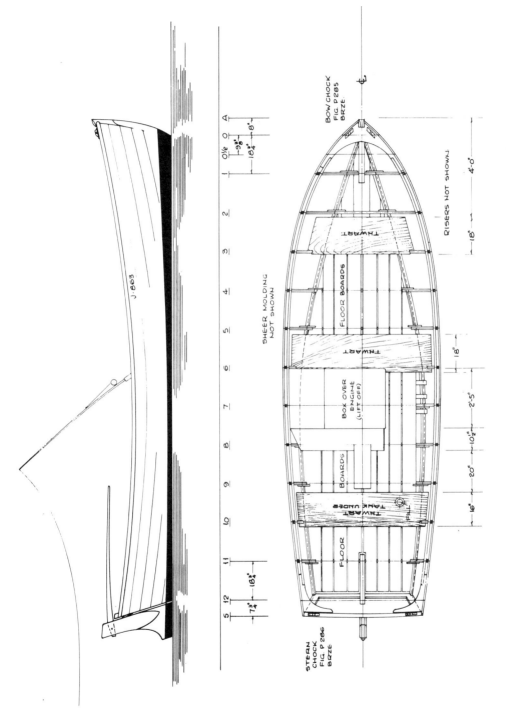

Profile and arrangement of the 20-foot Tom Davin reflect a practical boat. She is simple and a joy to own — the kind of boat the author intends to have built.

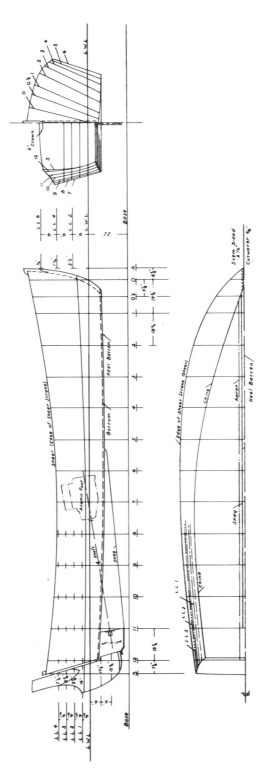

Lines of the Tom Davin. Her beam/length ratio is relatively low.

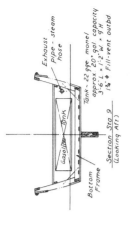

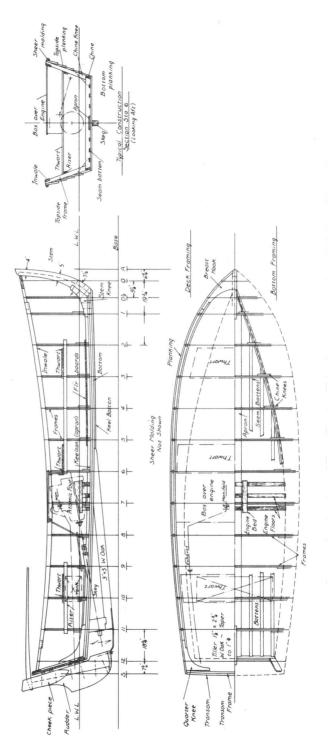

Scantlings
Stem & Stem Knee - Sided 2¼" - Molded as shown - W. Oak
Apron or Keelson - 7/8" x 8" W. Oak.
Transom - 7/8" W. Cedar - Transom Frame 7/8" x 3" W. Oak
Transom Knee - Sided 1 7/8" W. Oak.
Skeg - Sided 3" as shown - W. Oak
Keel Batten 7/8" x 3" W. Oak - 3/16" Bronze Strap forward as Cutwater covering jib end.
Bottom Planking - 7/8" W. Cedar.
Seam Battens - 5/8" x 1 7/8" W. Oak.
Topside Planking - 3/4" W. Cedar - 5 strakes each side
Side Frames - Sided 1 1/8" Molded 2¾" at chine - Taper to 1¾" at Inwale, W. Oak
Bottom Frames - Sided 1 1/8" Molded 2¾" W. Oak
Chine - 1 1/8" x 2½" W. Oak single length
Chine Knees - ¾" W. Oak or 5/8" Bruynzeel M'h'gy plywood
Inwale - 7/8" x 2½" W. Oak - Saw forward portion to shape Take template from work - Scarf join
Sheer Molding - 1¾" H.R. W. Oak - Saw forward portion to template taken from work. Ideally single length but may be scarf joined
Quarter Knees & Breasthook - 1¼" W. Oak laminated
Risers - ¾ x 2½ W. Oak. Thwarts - ¾" Mahogany or Cedar
Floor Boards - ½" W. Cedar
Engine Beds - Sided 1¾" W. Oak - Take molded dimensions from lofted lines
Engine Floors - Sided 1 5/8" W. Oak. Fasten thru bottom
Rudder - 1 1/8" Mahogany - Taper at edges
Cheek Pieces ¾" W. Oak. Dowel with 5/16" brze rod
Bronze shoe & rudder hangers
Engine Box - ½" Bruynzeel plywood - oak frame 5/8" x 2"
Exhaust pipe - steam hose
Gasoline Tank
Bottom Frame
Tank - 22 gge monel approx. 20+ gal. capacity 3'-6" L x 1'-2" W. x 9" H
1¾" Φ Fill-vent outbd
Section Sta 9
(Looking Aft)
Cheek piece
Rudder
L.W.L.
Thwart
Riser
Tank
Skeg
3" x 5" W. Oak
Man
Atomic Four
Thwart
Keelson (apron)
Frames
Inwale
Thwart
Fir boards
Keel Batten
Bottom
Stem
Stem Knee
Base
S 12 11 10 9 8 7 6 5 4 3 2 1 0½ 0 A
7¼" 18¾"
19¾" 9⅜" 6¼"
Sheer Molding Not Shown
Inwale
Box over Engine
Sheer molding
Topside frame
Thwart
Riser
Topside planking
Apron
Chine Knee
Chine
Seam batten
Skeg
Bottom planking
Typical Construction
Section Sta 6
(Looking Aft)
Planking
Deck Framing
Quarter Knee
Transom
Transom Frame
Exhaust
Tiller 1 1/8" x 2¾" W. Oak ~ Taper to 1" Φ
Thwart
Box over engine
Manifold
Thwart
Thwart
Breast Hook
Battens
Engine Bed
Engine Floors
Apron
Seam Battens
Chine Knees
Bottom Framing
Frames

Construction drawings of Tom Davin. *Using batten seams on the underbody and lapstrake topsides is practical construction.*

Tom Davin with Pat Atkin aboard the author's 26-foot We're Here. *Tom was a most inspiring man.*

Atomic Four engine is shown for power. Some other similar gasoline engine would work well, but I would not use a diesel in her, as these machines tend to vibrate and her flat bottom might tend to pant excessively. (Most small diesel engines do more than their share of vibrating and have to be installed carefully and mounted on flexible pads — all of which makes for complications.)

The lines show a relatively narrow hull with a fine entrance — much in the manner of many of the successful flat-bottomed boats my father and I have designed.

Batten seams are shown in her bottom, with lapstrake topsides — a combination that is hard to beat. While waterproof plywood can be used, my own boat will be constructed as shown.

Tom Davin will make a fine fishing boat for shoal areas, since the propeller and the heel of the rudder are protected by the keel and shoe. She will pound when going into a short chop, but, all things considered, *Tom Davin* will provide fine performance. She will behave herself in deep water and long swells, and she'll otherwise come up to all expectations, as has been proven over the years with similar hulls.

20

—— Amos Brown ——

22-foot 4¾-inch V-bottomed sloop

Seldom have I had the opportunity to design a boat purely without the influence of a client, but *Amos Brown* is such a craft — one designed just for fun and for this book.

While she may not look it, the boat was developed from Jake Hess's schooner *Florence Oakland. Amos Brown* evolved as I removed the schooner's billethead and trailboards and laid in a conventional stem. I feel that the result is an attractive — if not altogether practical — tabloid cruising boat. Her freeboard amidships is low and the trunk cabin is relatively low. Together, these features destroyed any possibility of sitting headroom. To overcome this, I borrowed a page from an early Stone Horse auxiliary with a trunk cabin and have shown sprung battens covered by a removable canvas. Without the "house top," one has the heavens for a ceiling and loses all concern about headroom of any kind.

The arrangement of *Amos Brown* includes berths port and starboard. A white enameled bucket equipped with a comfortable seat is tucked between these, and, while the bucket may not conform to present EPA regulations, it makes for a much more simple life.

The boat's galley is located at the companionway opening, with a sink

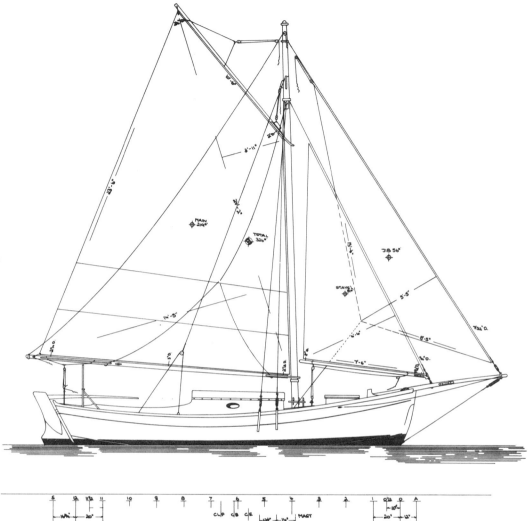

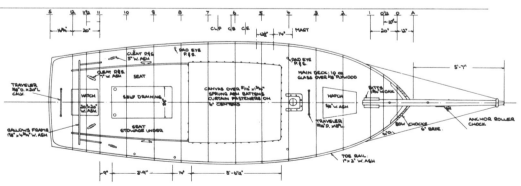

Sail plan and deck arrangement of the little hooker Amos Brown — *a boat designed for fun, without the influence of a client.*

Arrangement and construction plans of the 22-footer, with a section at station 6.

to port and a two-burner alcohol stove to starboard — both arranged in proper lockers. Indeed, her accommodations are quite nice for a 22-footer.

Her construction plan calls for ½-inch-thick waterproof plywood. (I have often used Permaply fir plywood with a phenol overlay and have had encouraging results.) Also specified is outside lead ballast — 1,200 pounds of it.

A self-draining cockpit and a bridge deck are included so that *Amos Brown* can venture offshore — naturally, under prudently chosen conditions, for she is a *little* boat! The sail area in the mainsail, staysail, and jib totals 326 square feet. I much prefer the low-aspect rig on all cruising boats, for, from my experience, it is easier to handle than the tall jibheaded rig of a racing machine.

Principal dimensions of *Amos Brown* are 22 feet 4¾ inches overall by 20 feet on the waterline by 7 feet 8 inches beam and 3 feet draft.

I named the 22-footer *Amos Brown* after the builder of the *James Samuel, Jr.* — in appreciation of his fine work and because there are all too few dedicated builders using wood in these days of fiberglass-reinforced plastic boats popped out of a mold!

21

—— Flipper ——

10-foot ½-inch flat-bottomed sailing skiff

In *The Book of Boats,* I wrote that *Mabel* is a famous little vessel. Her plans have been published the world over. They were first shown in *MotorBoat* magazine — affectionately known by many as "the old green sheet" — when Billy Atkin was doing a series of designs for that publication some 60 years ago! Later the design was presented in the well-loved magazine *Fore An' Aft* in an article by the late Weston Farmer. Still later, *Mabel* showed up in a 1937 book entitled *Motor Boats,* which was written by my father. He designed this little dinghy at Huntington, New York, in 1924.

Fairly recently, I revised the design of *Mabel,* after having built one of these boats in my Dinghy Shed. Based on my observations, I increased her freeboard and renamed her *Flipper.* The increased freeboard made a considerably more burdensome boat. The revised version, which is shown in the Appendix of Clem Kuhlig's book *Building the Skiff Cabin Boy,* has received favorable response.

Her principal dimensions are: 10 feet ½ inch overall by 3 feet 11 inches beam and 3½ inches draft.

Captain John Hart of Marblehead has built one of the boats. And Ken Rupprecht of Bristol, Rhode Island, did such a grand piece of work that

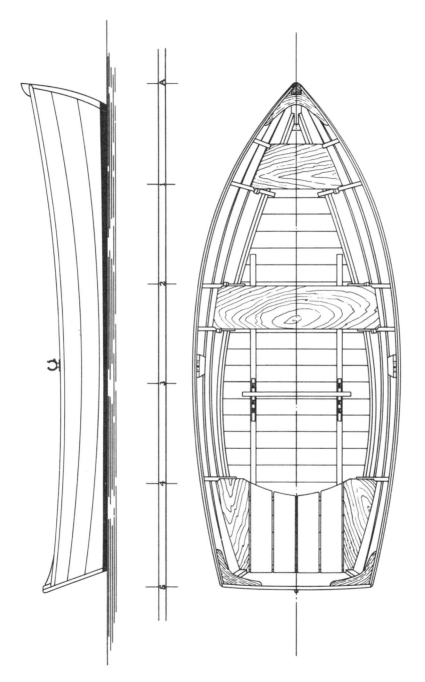

Flipper is a modification of Billy Atkin's famous Mabel, which was designed in 1924! Freeboard has been increased substantially and her sheer is "livelier" — but she is basically similar to the 60-year-old Mabel, which has been duplicated by many, many builders over the years. Principal dimensions are 10 feet ½ inch length overall by 3 feet 11 inches beam and 3½ inches draft.

Flipper *is nearing completion at Morehead City, North Carolina. Waterproof plywood has been used on the underbody of Charles McNeil's version of the rowing model. Her topsides frames are in the process of being notched and fitted. No athwartship frames were used, since they are not essential in relatively small boats. There is a jibheaded sail plan available for* Flipper.

his wife let him keep the boat in the living room! Charles McNeil of Morehead City, North Carolina, built a *Flipper* in the traditional manner except that he used a single sheet of waterproof plywood for the underbody. This technique can be used on any of the flat-bottomed boats described in this book. In some instances, it will be necessary to use athwartships bottom frames — or some other practical means of stiffening the underbody. But with a boat as small as *Flipper,* such reinforcement is not necessary.

There is an alternate arrangement for *Flipper* showing a jibheaded cat rig and daggerboard. She makes a fine training boat for youngsters — stable and dependable, with no need for a hiking strap or similar paraphernalia. It is time for a return to simplicity, and *Flipper* provides the opportunity.

22

—— Pollard 19 ——

19-foot fast powerboat

Some 20 years ago, Dick Pollard of East Hartford, Connecticut, asked me to design a practical, straightforward dayboat, and the *Pollard 19* was the result. Her principal dimensions are: 19 feet overall by 17 feet on the waterline by 7 feet 3 inches beam and 1 foot 7 inches draft.

The accommodations are limited: a space to change into swim trunks, modest facilities for overnight sleeping, and a comfortable cockpit for day cruising. These are combined with the boat's ability to travel at both low trolling speeds and a moderately fast clip under varying sea conditions.

Her construction is on the light side, with a full-length keel of white oak, sided 2½ inches. The propeller wheel is protected by a bronze shoe that runs aft and picks up the heel of the balanced spade rudder. Her station frames are Connecticut white oak, and planking is batten-seam Virginia white cedar. To provide for easy maintenance and all-around simplicity of operation, few complications are involved in her steering, engine, and other mechanical installations.

A 95 h.p., 6-cylinder Chris-Craft engine, direct drive, was installed for power. Finding the right engine will require investigations at the present time. Any well-built gasoline engine of similar displacement, weight, and

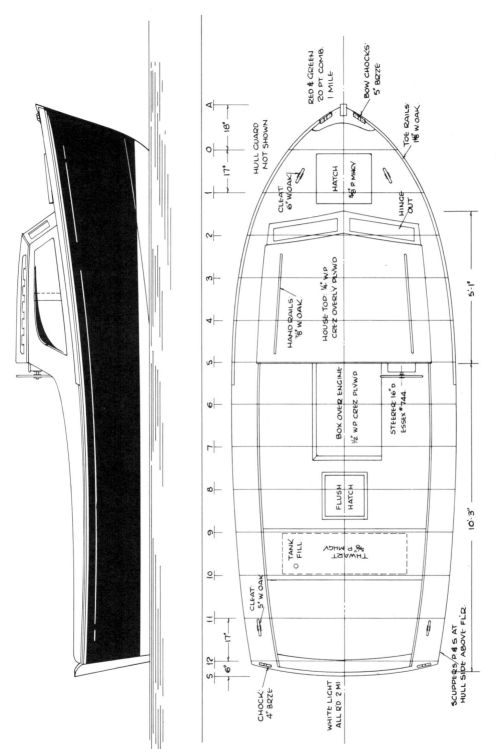

Profile and deck arrangement of Dick Pollard's 19-footer. She is primarily a day boat with a small cuddy incorporating two berths and a WC tucked on the centerline between these.

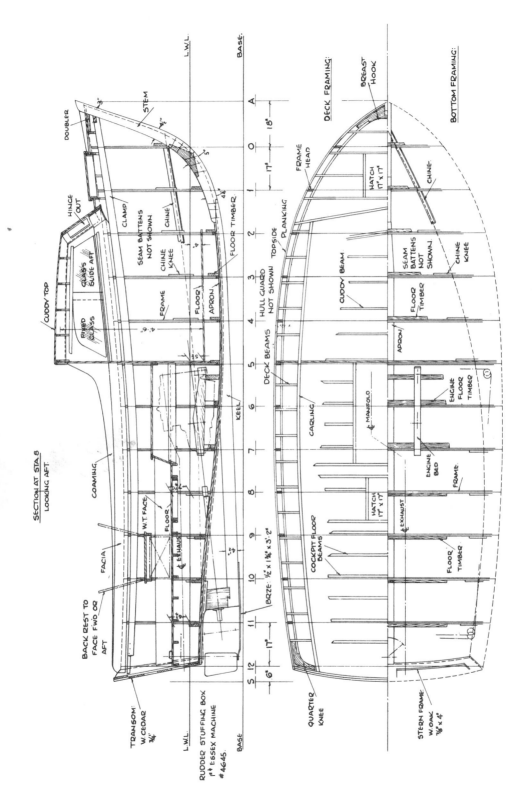

Construction drawings of the Pollard 19, which was built at East Hartford in 1958.

Pollard 19 *underway on the Connecticut River. The boat was clocked at 28.7 m.p.h. with a 95 h.p. Chris Craft 6-cylinder engine. She is sliding along with a minimum of fuss.*

horsepower will provide good results. I do not know, offhand, of a diesel engine that will do the same job without doing more than its share of vibrating. With the 95 h.p. Chris-Craft, she was clocked at 28.7 m.p.h. over a measured course. Thus, the *Pollard 19* has the distinction of being the fastest boat in this book.

Her cockpit is self-draining, the floor being some 7 inches above the waterline at station 8 and pitched aft from the cuddy bulkhead. There is sufficient depth in the cockpit and coamings to provide the occupant with security. An athwartships seat is fitted with a backrest that may be used on either the forward or the after side. This seat is placed forward of the transom to provide a comfortable position for trolling with one's feet braced against the inboard face of the transom.

The cuddy includes berths to port and starboard with a head between them on the centerline. Headroom here is 4 feet 6 inches under the beam. The forward hatch has a clear opening of 17 inches square and offers a secure place to stand when handling lines or anchoring.

Dick Pollard did fine work in the process of building his *Pollard 19*. It is encouraging to be able to assure any builder that the boat will come up to all expectations — provided that she is built in accordance with the working plans and a suitable power plant is installed.

23

—— Wild Onion ——

18-foot V-bottomed sloop

My father designed the 18-foot gaff-headed flat-bottomed sharpie *Red Onion* in May 1938. Three months later, he designed the 18-foot jib-headed sloop-rigged skipjack *Wild Oats*.

In 1982 I designed the 18-foot jibheaded skipjack *Wild Onion* in an attempt to improve the appearance of these little hookers — which should not be hard for anyone to do!

Both *Red Onion* and *Wild Oats* produced many (meaning ''a raft of,'' as Billy Atkin wrote in 1938) letters.

Billy Atkin wrote about *Red Onion* in 1968: ''Many years ago a friend of mine built a big flat-bottomed sailing skiff, built her as the work progressed without plans or model, and when she was finished, she did not look just right. A little off here and there, a lot cockeyed along her sheer. In the water she looked even worse than on land. Her owner christened her *Red Onion*. Asked why, he replied, 'Every time I look at her she brings tears to my eyes.' Which she did in truth. One of the world's worst-looking boats. And, sad to relate, after 30 years *Red Onion* is still being used — still bringing tears to the eyes of all who see her. Her name has always interested me — honest, plain, and forthright. Just the thing for a

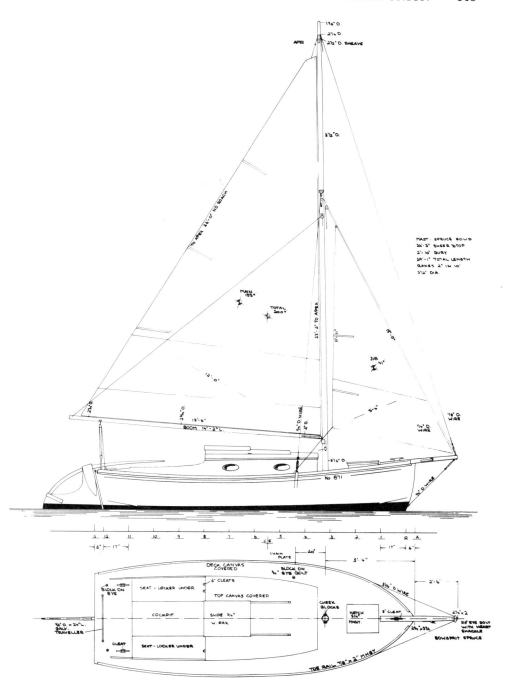

Sail and deck plan of the 18-foot Wild Onion. *She is based on the design of* Wild Oats, *designed by the author's father in 1938. The author has attempted to improve her appearance by increasing the sheer and changing other minor details.*

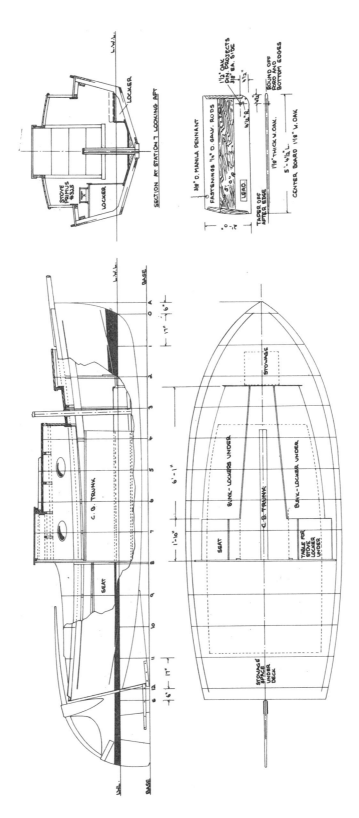

Arrangement plan and elevation of the Wild Onion. She is a simple tabloid cruising boat with a lot of ability.

Minka, *built from the plans of* Red Onion *by Richard Smith at Eugene, Oregon. He used the jibheaded rig of* Wild Oats, *and if you are confused, so am I!*

useful little hooker made for use and not for style. Just right for the last of our fleet. So, herewith, Shipmates, another *Red Onion.*''

Over the years, as I periodically pulled out the tracings of *Red Onion* and *Wild Oats,* I felt it would be a fun sort of challenge to see what I could do to maintain the basic concept yet create a boat that didn't quite bring tears to your eyes. Thus, here is *Wild Onion.*

Her principal dimensions are: 18 feet overall by 17 feet on the waterline by 7 feet beam and 1 foot 3 inches draft — precisely the same as *Wild Oats.*

I increased her sheer, which is an improvement, and I altered the shape and position of the deadlights in the trunk sides. There is 4-foot sitting headroom either side of the centerboard trunk, and she will carry 300 pounds of inside ballast.

The deckline is full, a feature that permits wholesome flare above the chines. While it is more difficult to build the boat this way, it will be well worth the extra effort.

I hope my *Wild Onion* doesn't bring tears to your eyes. If she is built in accordance with her working drawings, I suspect she will bring you lots of enjoyment.

24

——Awake——

13-foot 11-inch Swampscott rowing dory

The rowing boat *Awake* is an excellent sort of boat for use in either salt water or fresh water. The boat is well suited for most kinds of fishing, especially trolling for striped bass and other fish that feed in shallow water.

Awake was designed primarily for rowing, and she will row very easily. A small outboard motor can be used for power, but it should not be more than 2½ or 3 h.p.

The principal dimensions of this modified dory are 13 feet 11 inches overall by 12 feet on the waterline by 4 feet 4½ inches beam and 4 inches draft. Freeboard is an even 2 feet at the bow and 1 foot 5 inches at the stern. If built to the scantlings indicated, the finished boat will weigh about 150 pounds.

The lines drawing illustrates a conventional dory like those made famous around Swampscott, Massachusetts. The flat bottom has a slight amount of rocker, the bilges are rounded, and the planking is lapstrake. The ample flare ensures dryness and provides reserve buoyancy. *Awake* was designed for rowing, so if she is pushed at much more than 8 miles per hour, the bow will rise and the stern will settle.

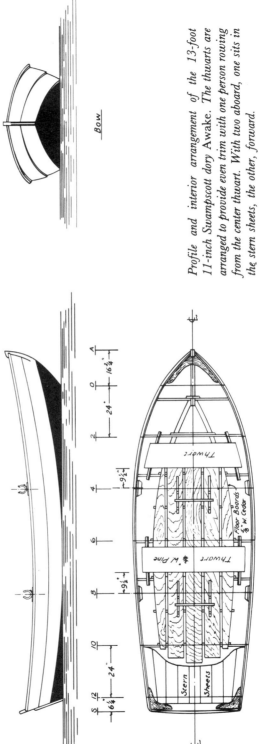

Profile and interior arrangement of the 13-foot 11-inch Swampscott dory Awake. The thwarts are arranged to provide even trim with one person rowing from the center thwart. With two aboard, one sits in the stern sheets, the other, forward.

Bow

Thwart

Thwart ½" W. Pine

Floor Boards ⅝" W. Cedar

Stern Sheets

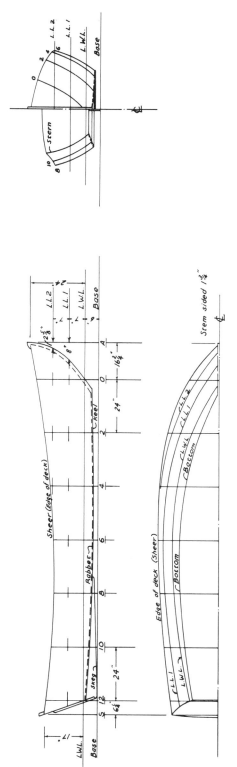

The lines in the profile, plan, and section must be laid down full size before starting to build.

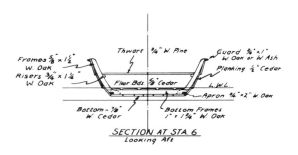

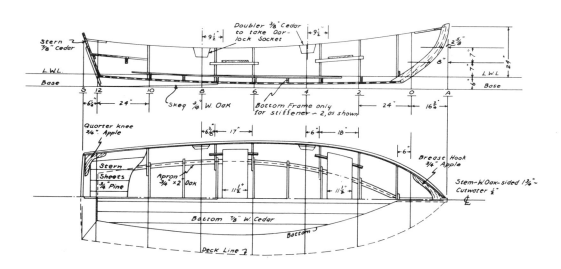

Construction drawings for Awake, with a section at station 6. The boat will be an ideal training boat for camps and other waterfront facilities.

Captain John S. Hart, at Marblehead, Massachusetts, built Awake *and named her* Benji's Boat. *Benji is in the stern sheets, and John's daughter-in-law Donni Hart is resting her oars.*

Unlike the bottom of the usual Bank dory, that of *Awake* is relatively wide. This increases the stability considerably. All dories (including the narrow-bottomed Bank dories) are excellent boats, able and easy to row. Nonetheless, the modified Swampscott dory, with its wider bottom aft, is more stable initially. The Bank dories have low initial stability when empty and require a cargo of fish — or proper ballasting — to provide stability. Thus they are not as practical for all-around use as a boat like *Awake*.

Rowing continues to grow in popularity and is both grand exercise and a rewarding means of keeping in shape. *Awake* will be excellent for the sport, for she is very well balanced and tucked up sufficiently to slide through the water easily.

There have been a great many dory designs over the years, but there is always room for another approach to the design — one that is not too difficult or expensive to build to meet the needs of the many people in search of a simple, practical boat.

25

— Petey Dink CM —

6-foot 6-inch round-bottomed pram

My father designed *Petey Dink* and named her *Katydidn't*. The design is included in his book *Motor Boats,* published by The Macmillan Company in 1937. In this he wrote, "One needs a dinghy that will be towed most of the time — but occasions arise when it becomes best to get the dink on deck or in the cockpit. I know of no other plans for a dinghy so small as this and so economical to build in the amateur workshop, or have built professionally. Mr. W.J. McElroy has had a *Katydidn't* built by Ole Amondsen at Greenwich. It seems to be entirely satisfactory, rows well with one or two aboard — and will carry three in smooth water.

"Now in such a tiny boat as this, there is no way in which to correct violent changes in trim caused by passengers — the weight of the load is out of all proportion to the displacement of the boat. So don't anticipate rowing off to sea in her. *Katydidn't* is not a rowing boat — rather, she is the smallest practical boat in which to get ashore from or aboard a cruiser. Nor will she sail — and by the same token she is not a life boat.

"*Katydidn't* is a round-bilge pram-type dinghy, and is of a size that can be towed without effort, lifted aboard if necessary, and is so light as not to require a giant to move her about. The length is 6 feet 6 inches, the breadth is 3 feet 4 inches, and her draft is 3½ inches.

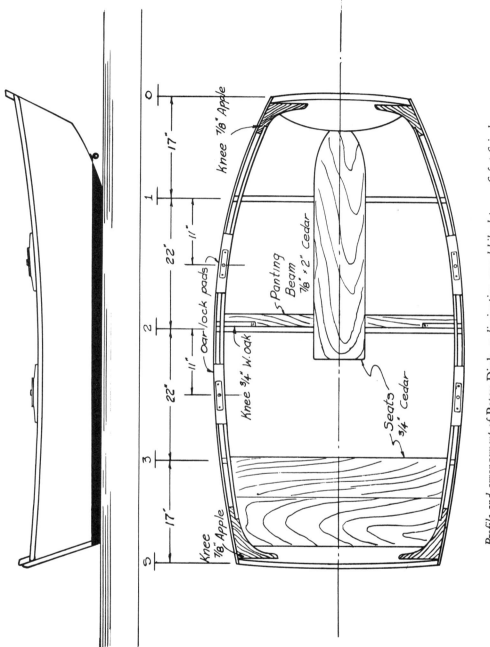

Profile and arrangement of Petey Dink, a diminutive, round-bilged pram, 6 feet 6 inches long overall. She is not a "rowing boat"; rather, she is the smallest practical boat to use in getting to or from an anchored sailing boat or power cruiser.

Knee 7/8" Apple

Oar-lock pads

Panting Beam 7/8" × 2" Cedar

Knee 3/4" W.Oak

Seats 3/4" Cedar

Knee 7/8" Apple

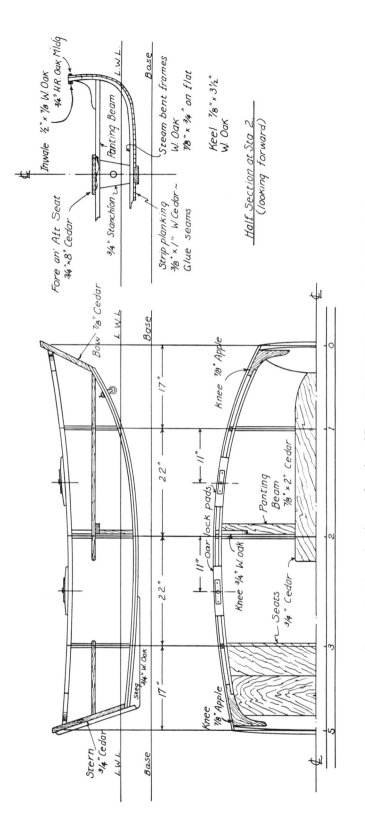

Construction plan, elevation, and section of Petey Dink. White-cedar strip planking, ⅜-inch thick by 1 inch wide with glued seams, constitutes her skin. Only three frames are required, since the finished hull is a monocoque structure capable of maintaining its own shape. This is a "flat-floored," round-bottomed model with considerable inherent stability. Her total weight, built as designed, will be about 60 pounds.

Inwale ½" x ⅞ W. Oak
¾" H.R. Oak Mldg.

Fore an' Aft Seat
¾"x 8" Cedar

Panting Beam

¾" Stanchion

Strip planking
⅜" x 1" W. Cedar —
Glue seams

Steam bent frames
W. Oak
⅞" x ¾" on flat

Keel ⅞" x 3½"
W. Oak

Half Section at Sta. 2
(looking forward)

Bow ⅞" Cedar

L.W.L.

Base

Knee ⅞" Apple

Oar lock pads

Panting
Beam
⅞" x 2" Cedar

Knee ¾" W. Oak

Seats
¾" Cedar

Skeg ¾" W. Oak

Stern
¾" Cedar

Base

L.W.L.

Knee
⅞" Apple

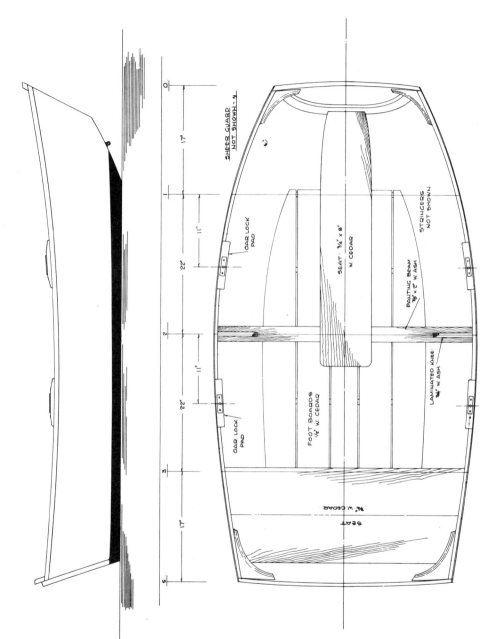

Profile and arrangement of Petey Dink CM. There are two sets of rowlocks to maintain trim with different crew numbers. The towing eye is tucked under the forward overhang; a towline secured in this position will tend to lift the bow.

SHEER GUARD
NOT SHOWN

OAR LOCK
PAD

SEAT: ¾' x 8"
W. CEDAR

PAINTING BEAM
⅞" x 2" W. ASH

STRINGERS
NOT SHOWN.

FOOT BOARDS
¼" W. CEDAR

LAMINATED KNEE
¾" W. ASH

OAR LOCK
PAD

SEAT
¾" W. CEDAR

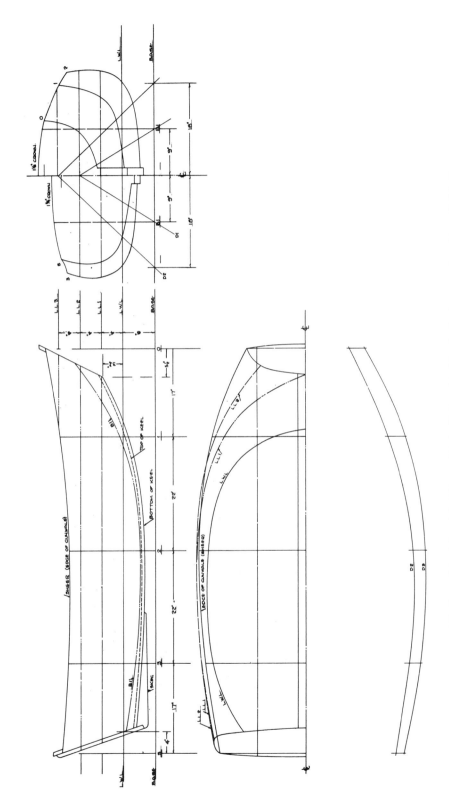

The lines of the 6-foot 6-inch Petey Dink CM are ideal for the development of a cold-molded hull.

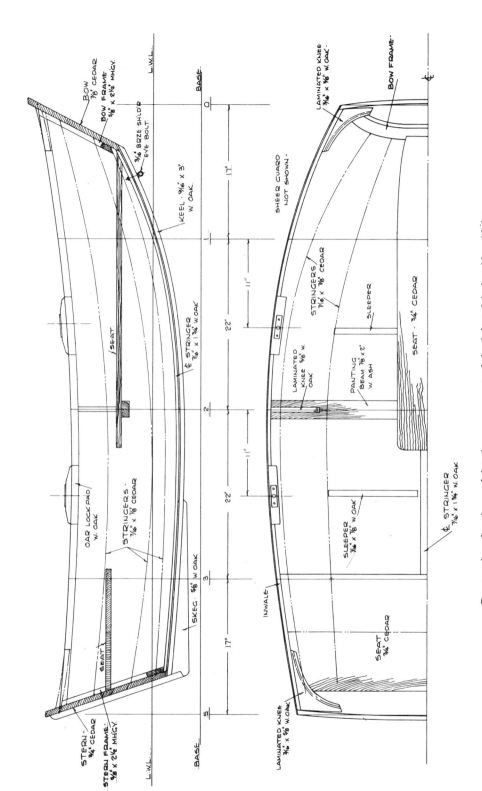

Construction elevation and interior arrangement of the 6-foot 6-inch cold-molded pram
Petey Dink CM.

Wilbur McElroy drew this lovely little sketch of Petey Dink *sloshing along astern of a modest auxiliary. What more could anyone ask in the way of peace and contentment?*

"There is an after seat. The other extends fore and aft and is supported on the bow and on a stanchion and panting beam amidships. Thus, the oarsman, by shifting from the after to the forward pair of rowlocks, maintains trim with one, two, or even three persons aboard, but it will be like subway crowding with three aboard.

"*Katydidn't* is flat-floored, of the round-bottom model, and in smooth water will carry just three average-weight people, and two in reasonable safety."

My *Petey Dink CM* is a modified version of *Katydidn't*. I increased her sheer and freeboard forward and aft. In all other respects, my father's description of her in *Motor Boats* applies.

I have also changed her construction from a strip-planked hull to one incorporating cold-molding — the WEST System. I did this to enable builders interested in this method to experiment with a rather small boat — and an equally small, or modest, investment.

The hull is shown constructed of three thicknesses of $\frac{1}{16}$-inch mahogany, laid diagonally at 45 degrees, and epoxy saturated. Her keel is $\frac{9}{16}$-inch white oak and there are three $\frac{7}{16}$-inch by $\frac{7}{8}$-inch white cedar stringers, in addition to a centerline stringer inboard of the keel.

There are several texts available on the building of cold-molded hulls, and any of the well-proven methods can be followed. I recommend John Guzzwell's *Modern Wooden Yacht Construction,* published in 1979 by International Marine. (The developers of the WEST System also have written a book on the subject — *The Gougeon Brothers on Yacht Construction.*)

I have also included plans for the original strip-planked method. This version is simply named *Petey Dink,* for builders who want to try their hand at this type of construction. The offsets of the two boats vary at points, so it is necessary to decide right at the outset which of the two boats to build.

26

—— Handy Andy ——

8-foot round-bottomed sailing dinghy

My father designed *Handy Andy* in 1924 when we lived in Huntington, New York. Here is what he wrote about this little round-bilged tender:

"There are no two men who like exactly the same kind of boat, and when it comes to the dink — well, there are lots of different kinds. This is perhaps because the man who owns a big motor cruiser has quite different service in view than the man who owns a tiny auxiliary. And the man who owns a houseboat sees the thing in a different light than the fellow who has a straight sailing craft. And so while one kind of dink may be excellent for one ship, it is all wrong for another. Thus the dinghy problem is admittedly difficult of solution, and the only thing to do is to design a lot of different types so that one or another of them will be just what you are looking for.

"*Handy Andy* is only 8 feet in length but with her generous freeboard and 4 feet of beam, she is a big little boat. By actual test she can carry four full-grown men, and three of the same is a comfortable load for her. Under the urge of a pair of 5½-foot spruce oars she travels easily, she is good under sail, and quite all right with an outboard motor hitched astride the stern board. The construction is light, which is a big advantage

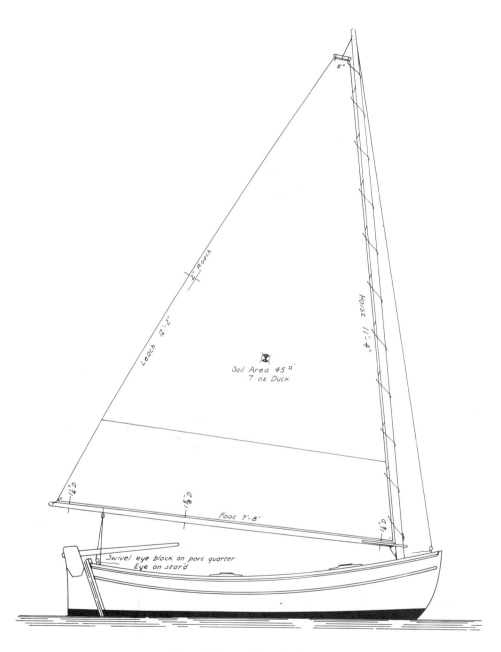

The sail plan of Handy Andy.

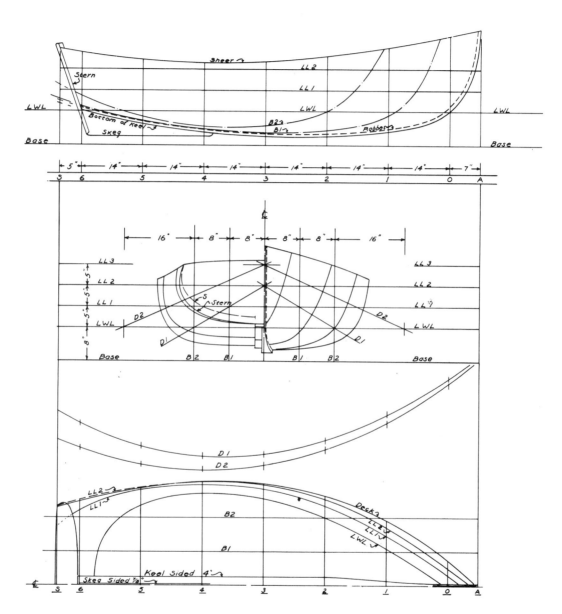

Lines drawings of Handy Andy, *the 8-foot round-bottomed "dink" designed by Billy Atkin in 1924.*

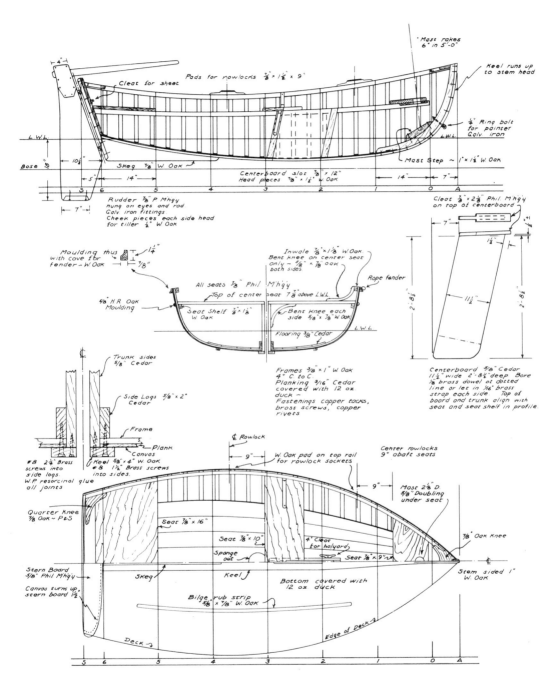

Complete construction details for the 8-foot sailing dinghy Handy Andy. *This was the original Penn Yan canvas-covered dinghy.*

Handy Andy *in our backyard at Huntington, about 1924. I am sitting amidships and my late brother, William W. Atkin, is in the stern. I've been exposed to boats, one way or another, for a very long time!*

in any dink that is to be used with a small cruiser. She will weigh less than 90 pounds with oars and fittings, but without the rig.

''The canvas-covered construction shown in the plans has proved successful in hundreds of thousands of canoes, and, besides being absolutely watertight, is stronger than a lightly built boat planked with wood and not so covered. The building of a boat of this description is not difficult, as the thin planks are easily applied and it makes little difference whether the butts are perfectly fitted because the canvas covering seals the bottom absolutely watertight anyway.

''There is a feeling among boating people to get back to sails, and there is no better way to master the art of sailing than in a little boat. There is a lot of fun to be had in puttering about the fleet in a sailing dink, a lot to be learned as well, and many are the hours when there is a gentle breeze and plenty of time to sail.''

Let me tell you more about *Handy Andy.* She was the design for the original Penn Yan canvas-covered dinghy, and hundreds of boats were built from this design. They have, in fact, become something of a classic.

During World War II, we were asked by the Winner firm, in Trenton, New Jersey, to prepare a proper dinghy for the PT boats. My father pulled out the drawings of *Handy Andy,* redesigned her after sections to eliminate the tumblehome, and the Winner firm built the boats. When the boats were delivered to the Navy Department, they were delighted with their performance. One of the admirals declared, ''It was one of the finest little boats they had ever seen.''

That is, briefly, the story of *Handy Andy.*

27

—— James Samuel, Jr. ——

17-foot 1-inch flat-bottomed catboat

Milton Bond of Fairfield, Connecticut, saw the design of *James Samuel* in an issue of *The Small Boat Journal* and decided that she was just what he wanted — except that he needed a smaller version that he could store in his garage. How often it is that a boat is just a little too big — or a little too small. There is no end to this business of boats!

Milton asked me to redesign the 20-footer, so I developed *James Samuel, Jr.* She is 17 feet 1 inch overall by 16 feet on the waterline by 7 feet 1 inch beam and 6½ inches draft. She is still a burdensome flat-bottomed skiff of good proportions, and quite capable of carrying Milton and his family off on picnics and daysails.

James Samuel, Jr. was built at the inland boatshop of Amos Brown in North Branford, Connecticut, and she is a fine piece of work. The boat is constructed in a traditional manner — planked smooth on her topsides and athwartships on the bottom. Rotary-cut Bruynzeel plywood, ¾ inch, works out nicely and is practical.

There is 138 square feet of sail area in her cat rig. The sail is synthetic tanbark. The mast has been arranged in a tabernacle to allow Milton to lower the rig and poke into shallow waters, away from the busy harbors we are obliged to contend with these days. There is a lot to be said for this

Sail plan and arrangement of the 17-foot clamming skiff James Samuel, Jr., *designed for Milton Bond of Fairfield, Connecticut.*

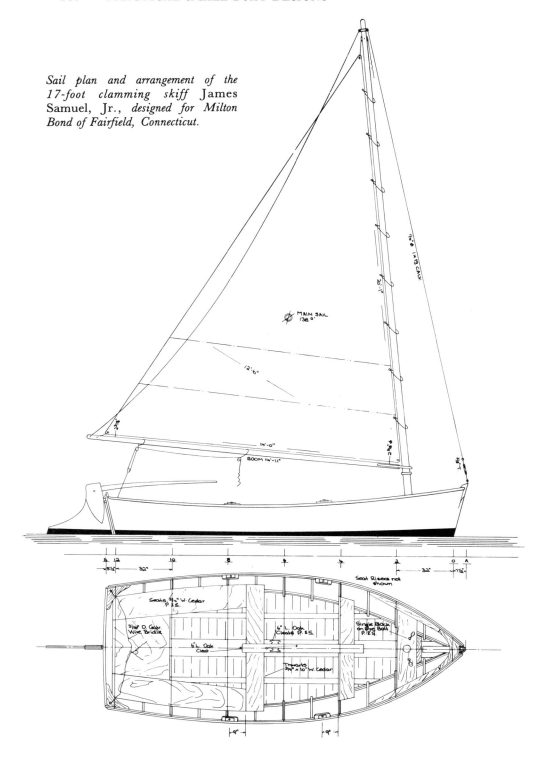

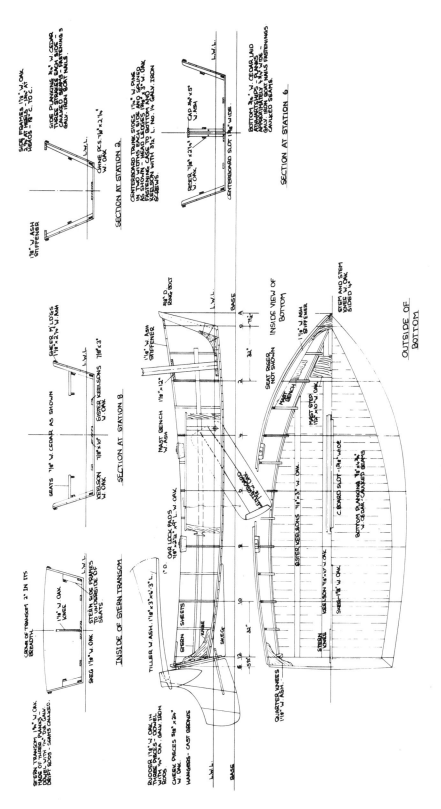

Construction elevation, plan, and sections of the James Samuel, Jr.

James Samuel, Jr. *nearing completion at the shop of Amos Brown, North Branford, Connecticut. What a fine piece of small-boat building! (Susan Brown photo)*

flexibility. Because of the tabernacle, it is necessary to rig shrouds. Otherwise, the mast would require only the single headstay.

Milton's hull has been painted white, the trim has been left bright, and the interior is mast buff — just the right scheme for a boat of this nature.

A 3 h.p. long-shaft British Seagull outboard is mounted on a bracket to port of the large rudder.

Let there be no doubt that *James Samuel, Jr.* is a big boat. A big, practical skiff for those who enjoy exploring the backwaters and shallows of our coast.

28

— Sedge* —

15-foot 3-inch flat-bottomed outboard

Modest in dimensions, modest in pretension, modest in cost — that describes *Sedge*. She is a very little boat for use in many, many places, such as along river levees or through the sedge that stands waist-deep in salt water. She can be used, in fact, in any protected waters. That punt-shaped bow can be nosed onto a shelving beach or a river bank.

Despite her squareness, *Sedge* will not be bad in reasonably rough water. But few small boats can be expected to wallow through a high sea. It has always been my advice, for that matter, to keep an eye on the weather in the handling of boats of any kind.

With a tentlike awning to cover the forward end of the cockpit, a couple of hardy souls might cruise in comparative comfort. For this purpose, the forward thwart can be made removable, leaving more than a full-length floor for an air mattress.

Sedge will drive easily up to 10 m.p.h.; 8 m.p.h. is her best speed, and this requires only modest power. The choice of a suitable outboard motor is so much a matter of personal preference that I shall not specify one. The dotted outline shown on the profile drawing is purely a sketch, and, except for being of approximate size, it does not represent any particular motor.

---

* *The design of* Sedge *is published with permission of Hearst Marine Books, New York.*

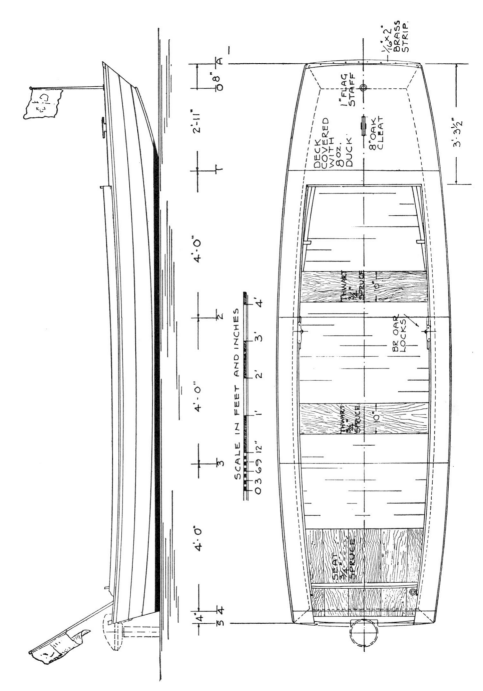

8"

A

2'-11"

T

4'-0"

4'-0"

3

SCALE IN FEET AND INCHES

0 3 6 9 12"   1'   2'   3'   4'

2

4'-0"

4"
5

4

DECK
COVERED
WITH
8 OZ.
DUCK

1" FLAG
STAFF

8" OAK
CLEAT

⅟₁₆×2"
BRASS
STRIP.

3'-3½"

THWART
¾"
SPRUCE
9"

BR. OAR
LOCKS

THWART
¾"
SPRUCE
10"

SEAT
¾"
SPRUCE

Outboard profile and deck plan of the punt-nosed Sedge.

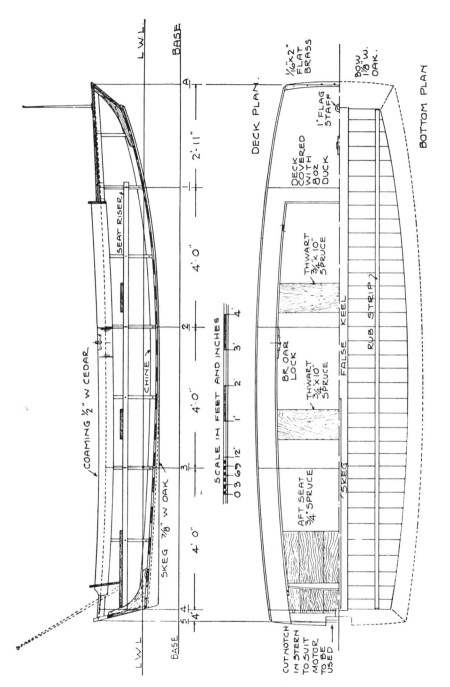

LWL

BASE

2'-11"

4'-0"

COAMING ½" W. CEDAR

SEAT RISER

CHINE

SKEG ⅞" W. OAK

4'-0"

4'-0"

3

2

1

SCALE IN FEET AND INCHES

0 3 6 9 12"   1'   2'   3'   4'

5

4
4'

BASE

LWL

DECK PLAN.

⅟₁₆"x2"
FLAT
BRASS

BOW
1⅜" W.
OAK.

DECK
COVERED
WITH
8 OZ
DUCK

1' FLAG
STAFF

BOTTOM PLAN

THWART
¾"x10"
SPRUCE

BROAR
LOCK

THWART
¾"x10"
SPRUCE

FALSE KEEL

SKEG

RUB STRIP

AFT SEAT
¾" SPRUCE

CUT NOTCH
IN STERN
TO SUIT
MOTOR
TO BE
USED

Construction plans of Sedge. The boat can be built of waterproof plywood without difficulty.

Sedge is 15 feet 3 inches overall, 12 feet on the waterline, 4 feet 7 inches beam, and 5 inches draft (without motor). The freeboard is 1 foot 5 inches at the bow and 1 foot 2⅞ inches at the stern. For a little boat, *Sedge* has ample freeboard; this, in combination with the flare on the topsides, will make a very dry boat. Flare is a most advantageous feature. It promotes stability as much as it creates dryness.

The arrangement shows a wide seat aft fitted with a lazy-back. If the seat and the lazy-back are watertight between the stern, the side, and the bottom of the lazy-back, any water that splashes into the cutout for the outboard's clamping device will simply flow back overboard.

The two thwarts should be placed as shown, being spaced for even loading. *Sedge* will easily carry four, but two is preferable — except in very still water. The short deck forward will be useful for stepping ashore and the space below will form a very welcome stowage area. Side decks contribute a large amount of strength. Without these, the hull is likely to wring and, consequently, leak.

The lines show a flat-bottomed model, easiest of all types to build. The bow is nearly as wide as the stern, and the deck line is curved only enough to give some form to the boat. The bottom has the correct rocker for the speed suggested, and it is essential to preserve this in construction. Too little or too much rocker will spoil the boat for use with modest power. When a boat is flat-bottomed, there is a tendency to be careless of the form, so in building *Sedge*, bear in mind that the most certain way to produce an unsatisfactory boat is to set up the centerline mold and the two ends and simply spring on the side planking.

I cannot stress enough the value of laying down the lines full size and making all the forms shown in the lines drawing. These should be set up as carefully as though this were a big ship. Then, when the boat is finished she will have been built as planned — and not by some rule-of-thumb process that will produce something that will float, but not something that will be a masterpiece.

My friend and shipmate William W. Holcombe of Newtown, Connecticut, built one of these boats some years ago. He powered her with a 6 h.p. outboard and was delighted with the results.

I have filled requests for plans of this little boat from people living far from the sea: in many towns along the Mississippi River and along the shores of small lakes. She is not too big or too heavy to move about on a simple trailer. The total weight without motor and equipment will be a little over 200 pounds, and two men can manage that.

Do not be tempted to pull the ends out, raise the sheer heights, snoop up the bow or the stern, or do the many tempting things a boat plan always impels one to do. Just put this very little boat together as she is planned and see how well she performs.

Sedge can be built successfully and practically of waterproof marine plywood — ½ inch on her underbody and ⅜ inch on her topsides.